Hollywood in World War II Delaware

Hollywood
IN
WORLD WAR II DELAWARE

MICHAEL J. NAZAREWYCZ

THE
History
PRESS

Published by The History Press
Charleston, SC
www.historypress.com

First published 2023

Manufactured in the United States

ISBN 9781467153805

Library of Congress Control Number: 2023934823

Notice: The information in this book is true and complete to the best of our knowledge. It is offered without guarantee on the part of the author or The History Press. The author and The History Press disclaim all liability in connection with the use of this book.

This book is dedicated to my wife, Judy;
to my daughters, Victoria and Veronica;
and to my late grandfather Charles L. Harrison

CONTENTS

PREFACE

See me now or see me later.

Of all the things my grandfather shared with me—far too many things to list here—it's this quote I think of frequently. When he spoke it, it was usually in the context of some kind of auto maintenance. If my car was due for an oil change or the tire pressure needed checking or some such thing, he would ask if I had taken care of it and I would usually say that I hadn't yet—because usually I hadn't yet—and he would say, "See me now or see me later." Change your oil today, or you'll have engine problems tomorrow. Check your tires today, or you'll have a flat tomorrow. Those instances were specific, but the broader lesson was clear, too: take care of things today or there may be problems tomorrow.

See me now or see me later.

I've used this quote throughout my life, mostly as a way to help my children understand the consequences of procrastination in school. But I've thought of it recently in other contexts, too, like my first book.

One of the great joys of writing *Historic Movie Theaters of Delaware* was having the chance to learn and document and share so much of the state's great history in an area about which I have much passion. But one of the challenges of writing that book was that as I learned things I didn't know before, I wanted to tell those stories as well, but I couldn't—they were either too detailed to fit within the book's broader narrative structure, too lengthy to fit within the book's word limit or too expansive to fully vet and write and edit before my deadline. Those stories involved Delaware and Hollywood and World War II.

That era-specific interest was inspired by the same grandfather. He was a veteran of the U.S. Navy—a member of the Seabees who served in the South Pacific in World War II. I thought a lot about him as I dug into the state's 1940s theater history for that book, wishing I could tell more of those stories but knowing I couldn't. And despite the legitimacy of those reasons, and despite how happy I was (and still am) with that book, I couldn't shake the notion of "see me now or see me later," only with a twist: *Historic Movie Theaters of Delaware* was my first book—the realization of a lifelong dream to be a published author—but the opportunity to write it did not guarantee the opportunity to write another someday.

"See me now or see me later" became "See me now, there might not be a later."

But I had to take that message's twist and twist it again. Where "see me now or see me later" was always a lesson in avoiding procrastination, I turned it into an exercise in patience. I got my chance to tell the original story I wanted to tell; I got my Now. What I needed next was everything else the first book required—work, discipline, confidence, orchestration, support, fortune—and add to it the patience to await the chance to tell the next story I wanted to tell.

Welcome to Later.

ACKNOWLEDGEMENTS

Organization Representatives

Air Mobility Command Museum: Eric S. Czerwinski
Corbit-Calloway Public Library (Odessa, Delaware): Library Staff
Delaware State Parks, Fort Delaware State Park/Fort DuPont State Park/Port Penn Interpretive Center: Jake Miller
Delaware Public Archives: The Mabel Lloyd Ridgely Research Room Staff
Newark Historical Society: Mary Torbey
Selbyville Public Library: Kelly Kline
Town of Bethany Beach Cultural and Historical Affairs: Carol Olmstead
Town of Millsboro: Matt Hall
University of Delaware Library, Special Collections: Curtis Small, PhD, MLIS

Individuals

Victoria Nazarewycz   Dotty Verne

The History Press

Abigail Fleming   Kate Jenkins   Crystal Murray

The fellows in this outfit had not seen a movie for three months until last night when they attended a show in the rest area. You people at home should have seen the sparkle come into their weary eyes to realize how much they enjoy a show. They sit right out in the cold for two hours and for that length of time they are able to forget all about this awful mess and just thank God they can forget for that long Jerry and shells and everything. Even as accustomed as I am to movies, having worked at a motion picture house, I find myself looking forward to a movie.

—*Private First Class George Giles, a former projectionist at Wilmington's Rialto Theatre, who entered the army to serve his country as a radio operator, in a letter to the* News Journal, *written around February 1945 from somewhere in Luxembourg*

THE HISTORY

From Opera Houses to Movie Palaces in the First State (1868 to 1939)

On July 27, 1868, almost twenty-six thousand days before Germany invaded Poland to start World War II, a ceremony was held in Middletown, Delaware, to celebrate the laying of the cornerstone of the Middletown Town Hall. On the second floor of the three-story town hall was the Middletown Opera House, which, over time, would evolve from a live entertainment house and community gathering spot to a full-on motion picture theater, cementing its place in history as the first theater built in Delaware to go on to show movies. That theater still exists today. It is now known as the Everett Theatre, and yes, it still shows movies.

From that point in 1868 and forward, the theater landscape in Delaware exploded. Over the next seventy years, the state would see a total of ninety-two theaters open in cities as far northeast as Claymont and as far southwest as Delmar (on the Delaware side, of course). In between? Town after town wanted and built their own opera houses, auditoriums and theaters: Bethany (three), Bridgeville (two), Claymont (one), Delaware City (three), Delmar (two), Dover (three), Ellendale (one), Frankford (one), Frederica (one), Georgetown (two), Greenwood (one), Harrington (three), Laurel (two), Lewes (three), Middletown (two), Milford (four), Millsboro (three); Milton (two), New Castle (four), Newark (five), Odessa (one), Rehoboth (two), Seaford (three), Selbyville (two), Smyrna (two), Wilmington (thirty-four).

Not every theater survived, of course. Of those ninety-two theaters to open in that seventy-year span, only thirty-nine were open as of the end of 1938, but that is still more than twice as many as were open at the turn of the century (nineteen). Then, in February 1939, Delaware's ninety-third theater overall and the fortieth theater to be open at the time, Wilmington's Warner Theatre, would be the last new Delaware theater to open before World War II began. That theater opening also closed an interesting set of prewar bookends.

When I spoke at the Delaware Public Archives after the release of *Historic Movie Theaters of Delaware*, I provided my "Top 10 Historic Delaware Theaters" list. There are a lot of great theaters that made that list, and maybe arguments can be made that others should have been included, but for my money, the top two will always be the top two.

At no. 1 is the Everett Theatre, the First State's first theater.

Something I suspect the members of the M.W. Grand Lodge of Delaware didn't realize as they laid that cornerstone of the Middletown Town Hall was that they were writing the prologue to a story not unlike a Hollywood epic.

It starts with humble beginnings on that second floor as little more than a large room with moveable chairs where the community could be entertained by the likes of touring opera troupes, traveling minstrels, local thespians and more. The Opera House even had something akin to a house band called the Amphions, which routinely provided music as needed. But it wasn't just about entertainment. The Opera House also served as a venue where the community could gather to tend to town business, like fundraisers, political rallies and school commencements.

As the nineteenth century progressed, so too did the Opera House and what it offered to Middletown and the surrounding region, including those aforementioned moving pictures that would be cornerstones of another kind—cornerstones on which the theater's movie house legacy would be built, although not right away.

Like the hero in a Hollywood epic, the Middletown Opera House had to first prove its resiliency, and it did that more than once. After fifty years of serving its community, the Opera House suffered a fate similar to its kin around the state: it was lost to fire. Undaunted, Middletown rebuilt its Opera House only to lose it to another fire four years later. But out of that second pile of ashes rose a new phoenix—the Everett Theatre. When the third incarnation of that gathering place in that same Main Street location was rebuilt in 1922, it was rebuilt with movies in mind first.

Throughout the 1920s and into the '30s, the Everett moved in step with the big-city theaters in Wilmington. It showed moving pictures, offered live entertainment, continued to serve as a community gathering place and went

The three-story building on the right is the original Middletown Town Hall; the Opera House is on the second floor (circa 1908). *GRA 138, Delaware postcard collection, Special Collections, University of Delaware Library, Museums & Press, Newark, Delaware.*

through its own technology upgrades when talking pictures became the Hollywood standard. But sometime around 1932, it closed, presumably for business purposes, only to reopen in 1934 under new ownership but keeping the Everett name.

From there, the Everett and its community would enjoy decades of use. Church services were held there, war bonds were sold there, live entertainment graced its stage, polio vaccines were administered there, movies were screened there and on and on. The theater also faced challenges during that time, from an NAACP boycott in 1956 to a shooting in 1975. Then, around 1979, it faced another closure, again presumably for business reasons. This would last until 1982, when it reopened again with its familiar name but with a focus on its live entertainment roots (although always with films on the calendar).

The second act of this epic peaked with Hollywood glory—literal Hollywood glory—when, in 1988, director Peter Weir and star Robin Williams descended on the First State to film *Dead Poets Society*, the first feature-length film to shoot entirely in Delaware. The ten-week shoot, which used town and regional locals as extras (many in high school and on Christmas break), spent the bulk of its time at Middletown's St. Andrew's

School and spots in Old New Castle. But a pivotal scene in the film, where Shakespeare's *A Midsummer Night's Dream* is performed onstage, was filmed at the Everett, which was refurbished specifically for the shoot. It seems poetic that Delaware's first theater to eventually screen films played a critical role in an actual film.

But that would not be the Everett's happily ever after. In March 2008, the ceiling collapsed, forcing its fifth closure (to recap: fire, fire, money, money, ceiling). But again, the theater and the community came through, and the refurbished place was back in business in May the following year, complete with an updated digital projection system to complement its classic twin Peerless 35mm projectors. Most recently, like all other theaters in the state, the Everett faced and overcame the challenges presented by measures implemented in response to the COVID-19 pandemic. As of this writing, the Everett still puts on shows and still shows movies.

This resiliency is a testament to not only the theater but also to the dedication and commitment of the residents of Middletown and neighboring Odessa and Townsend—three communities that combine to represent just 2.5 percent of the state's population, but whose passion for this historic place is as big as any city's in the state.

At no. 2, the state's last new prewar theater and one I considered seriously for the top spot: Wilmington's Warner Theatre.

It is impossible to say for sure if the Warner Theatre's 1939 opening was the most celebrated theater opening in the state's history, but it's at least in the conversation. There was plenty of glitz and many big-name locals at 210 West Tenth Street on the evening of February 8, including Mayor Walter Bacon, Lieutenant Governor Edward Cooch and city council president Albert James. Also in attendance was Jack Warner Jr. of the Warner family. Yes, *that* Warner family.

The Warners were no strangers to Wilmington. Prior to the flagship theater's opening, they already owned Wilmington's Garrick, Aldine, Arcadia and Queen theaters. In fact, the notion of an actual Warner Theatre, not just a theater owned by the Warners, may have begun as far back as 1930, when Pierre S. du Pont wrote a letter to Harry Warner asking for a theater to be built in Wilmington.

When the Warner opened, Lewis Black, who was already handling publicity and promotion for the city's Warner-owned theaters, was tapped to manage it. Months later, Black was named city manager for those theaters, and his star only rose from there as he became a leader in his industry and a pillar in his community, with bona fides covered later in this book.

This is the shell of what would become Wilmington's Warner Theatre (circa 1938). *Delaware Public Archives.*

The Warner Theatre cost $650,000 ($13.6 million today) and took two years to build, but when it was finished it was the largest theater in the state. With 1,550 seats on the main floor and 350 in the loge, its capacity was already formidable, but the lobby had room for an additional 1,000 people; another 750 could fit in the foyer. From a tech perspective, the theater was state of the art, with the same RCA Photophone equipment used at New York City's Radio City Music Hall. The building also boasted year-round air-conditioning, a first in Wilmington.

Over the years, because of the Warner name, the theater's stature and Black's excellence, the Warner Theatre became Hollywood's gateway to Delaware.

Appearances at the theater, along with public and private events organized by Warner or spearheaded by Black, included a dinner at the Hotel DuPont with former FBI agent turned writer Leon Turrou, on whose work the film *Confessions of a Nazi Spy* was based; an appearance at the theater by Howdy Doody's pal Clarabell the Clown; an appearance by the voice of Donald Duck, Clarence "Ducky" Nash; a speaking engagement by former first lady Eleanor Roosevelt; and even a dinner with actor Cary Grant.

Like many old theaters before it, the Warner slowly fell into disrepair, while newer theaters in the suburbs, where parking was not an issue and safety was less of a concern, grew in popularity. When the theater was sold in 1973, Black retired as its only manager to that point, a thirty-four-year run with a legacy that will never be matched.

Thus, bookends. The state's greatest theater and the state's most glamorous theater opened and closed the pre-World War II era of theatergoing in Delaware.

A little less than seven months after the Warner Theatre opened, Germany invaded Poland. The day before that is where this book begins.

THE THEATERS OF (PRE)WAR

Delaware's Movie Theater Landscape on August 31, 1939

The following is a listing of all Delaware movie theaters that were in business on August 31, 1939—the eve of Germany's invasion of Poland and the start of World War II. Where available, what each theater screened that night is listed.

ACE THEATRE, WILMINGTON. In March 1915, Wilmington's Polish section landed its first theater, the Polonia. The 350-seat theater specialized in Polish language films and religious pictures. After a 1922 closure, sheriff's sale and relocation, it became the Avenue Theatre and remained as such until 1936, when it became the Ace. Playing August 31, 1939: Action film *The Rookie Cop*, plus *Western Caravans* with B-western favorite Charles Starrett.

THE ALDINE | LOEW'S ALDINE, WILMINGTON. The Aldine wasted no time establishing itself when it opened in June 1921. The first film it screened was D.W. Griffith's *Dream Street*, with two of the film's stars, Ralph Graves and Charles Emmett Mack, appearing in person to promote the film. Two months before Pearl Harbor, a deal between Warner and Loew's converted the theater to Loew's Aldine. Playing August 31, 1939: *I Stole a Million*, a crime drama starring George Raft and Claire Trevor.

THE ARCADIA, WILMINGTON. When it opened in March 1921, this theater was originally going to be named the Princess Theatre, but the public was instead asked to vote on what the theater's name should be. The winning entry was the Wilart, but the owners didn't like that, so they went with the Arcadia instead. The theater was temporarily closed on August 31, 1939.

Armory Hall, Milford. Milford's Armory Hall had at least two iterations in its history. There is a news item that references an armory in 1884 and another cited as having opened in 1887. Throughout its history, before becoming the Shore Theatre in 1946, it played host to a long list of events, including film screenings.

The Auditorium, Wilmington. On what were previously circus grounds, the Auditorium was built in 1880 in response to the country's roller-skating craze. Like other multipurpose facilities around the state, the Auditorium was the sight of numerous entertainment attractions, including movies.

Ball Theatre, Millsboro. Of all of Delaware's theater owners (regardless of era), Walter "Huck" Betts, owner of the Ball Theatre, arguably has the most interesting background. Millsboro-born and raised, Betts had a childhood love for baseball. He had the skills too, and in 1920, at the age of about twenty-three, he was signed to pitch for the Philadelphia Phillies. After sixteen seasons around the majors and minors, Betts retired, came home and opened the Ball Theatre.

Blue Hen Theatre, Rehoboth. Likely Rehoboth's first movie theater, the Blue Hen started as the Casino Moving Picture Theatre (aka the Casino Photoplay) around 1909; it became the Blue Hen in 1914. During the World War II era, it was owned by Charles Horn, who would later sell it to William Derrickson.

Capitol Theatre, Dover. The Capitol Theatre is the state's second-oldest theatrical entity, having begun as the Dover Opera House (in two different locations) and later Nixon's Opera House. In 1930, owner Benjamin Shindler held a contest to rename the theater; it became the Capitol. Playing August 31, 1939: crime dramas *Blind Alley* with Chester Morris and Ralph Bellamy, and *Code of the Streets* starring Harry Carey and the Little Tough Guys.

Delmar Theatre, Delmar. In the southwest corner of the First State is Delmar, a town shared with the state of Maryland and dubbed "The Little Town Too Big for One State." What began as the Elcora Theatre in 1915 became the Delmar Theatre in 1935. Playing August 31, 1939: *The Kid from Kokomo*, a comedy with Pat O'Brien, Joan Blondell, Jane Wyman, Sidney Toler and Ward Bond.

Diamond Theatre, Selbyville. Raymond T. Quillin of Berlin, Maryland, who had already owned the Globe Theater in Berlin since 1926, built the Diamond Theatre in Selbyville in 1937.

Don Theatre | Pike Theatre, Claymont. In 1920, the Green Lantern Theatre, the first of several Claymont-based theaters in the state's history,

Ball Theatre, Millsboro (undated). *Photo by Robert F. Ferrier; courtesy of the Town of Millsboro.*

On the right side just beyond the DOLLY MADISON sign is the Diamond Theatre, Selbyville (undated). *Delaware Public Archives.*

opened in the northeast corner of Delaware. It closed around May 1939 and would not reopen as the Don Theatre until April 1940. It became the Pike Theatre in 1941.

Earle Theatre, New Castle. This theater began as the Royal Theatre in 1919, and over the next decade-plus, it evolved into the Elaine Theatre and the Colonial Theatre until 1933, when it settled into the Earle Theatre.

Everett Theatre, Middletown. See "The History: From Opera Houses to Movie Palaces in the First State (1868 to 1939)" for detailed information about the Everett and its beginnings as the Middletown Opera House. Playing August 31, 1939: the Irving Berlin musical *Second Fiddle*.

The Theater at Fort DuPont, Delaware City. Fort DuPont was the first of four Delaware military bases to offer moving pictures but the only one open at the start of World War II. There was no dedicated theater on the base when it opened in 1916; instead, films were screened in the Service Hut and would continue to be shown there for close to twenty years until a dedicated theater was built.

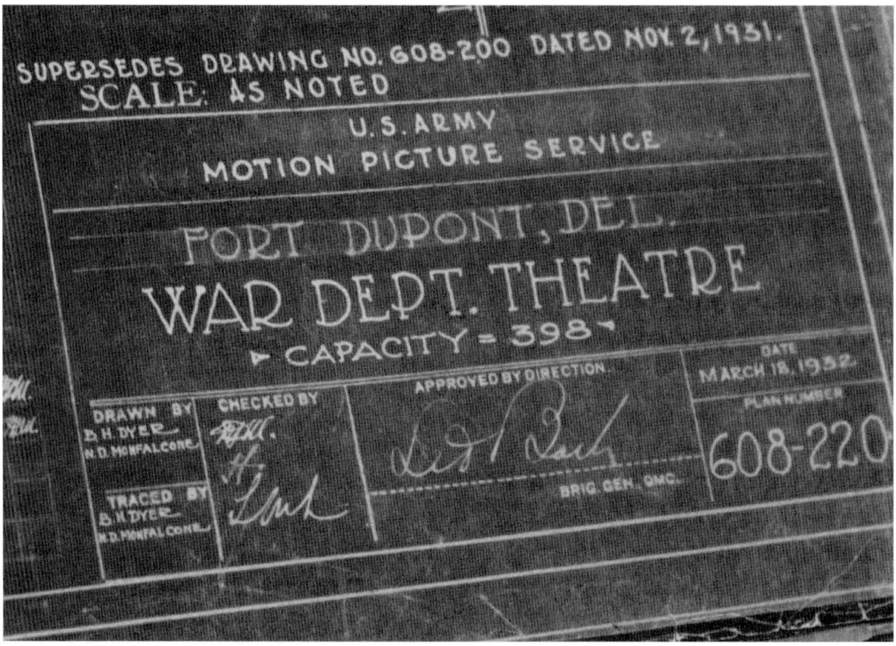

This portion of original blueprints from the Theater at Fort DuPont offers administrative details about the build (1931). A collection of original blueprints is part of the Fort DuPont archives. *Photo by Victoria Nazarewycz; photo produced with permission of the Delaware State Parks Cultural Resources Unit.*

GRAND THEATRE, WILMINGTON. It's interesting that while Wilmington would become the state's epicenter for the arts, in the early days of theaters, Middletown, Smyrna and Dover all had opera houses first. That changed with the opening of the Grand Opera House in December 1871. It's gone through slight name changes in its history, but "Grand" has always been a part of each name. Playing August 31, 1939: John Wayne in *Three Texas Steers*.

KELLER'S THEATRE, BRIDGEVILLE. Also known as the Bridgeville Theatre, Keller's Theatre opened in 1907 and was situated between the town's post office and fire hall. While open at the start of World War II, the theater would suffer a fiery fate in March 1941 and remain closed.

LEWES AUDITORIUM, LEWES. In June 1908, the cornerstone was laid for the Lewes Town Hall—a building not intended for government use, as was the case with most town halls, but rather for use by the public as the public saw fit. Within that hall was the Lewes Auditorium, which played host to a blend of vaudeville shows, local productions and moving pictures.

LOEW'S THEATRE | RITZ THEATRE, WILMINGTON. In January 1924, after the theater opened in 1921 as the Parkway Theatre, but before becoming the Adams' Parkway Theatre in December 1924, a private event of historical note took place here: the first sound screening in the city. The press had been invited to an exhibition of the Phonofilm, an audio/visual synchronization device that was the precursor to the Vitaphone. As for the theater itself, after other starts and stops, it became the Loew's Theatre in 1931 and finally landed as the Ritz Theatre in 1941. Playing August 31, 1939: the fine-looking duo of Robert Taylor and Hedy Lamarr in the drama *Lady of the Tropics*.

MILTON THEATRE, MILTON. In 1919, Ida Fox modified a room above her Union Street store for purposes of offering the town of Milton a theater. The Fox Theatre would be managed by her son, William, until his untimely passing later that same year. Ida took over the business and in doing so became one of the first female theater managers (possibly *the* first) in the state's history. A little more than a decade later, it became the Milton Theatre. Playing August 31, 1939: *You Can't Cheat an Honest Man*, featuring W.C. Fields along with Edgar Bergen and Charlie McCarthy. Screening with that was the crime comedy *For Love or Money*.

NATIONAL THEATRE, WILMINGTON. Although it was open to all, the National Theatre was the third (of four) and longest-lasting theater in Delaware's history to serve the Black community. It was built by Dr. Samuel G. Elbert, one of Delaware's first licensed Black physicians, in 1916. Playing August 31, 1939: Shirley Temple and Randolph Scott in *Susannah of the Mounties*.

NEW CASTLE OPERA HOUSE, NEW CASTLE. Opening in 1879, Delaware's fifth opera house was used as a rental hall and a roller rink in its early days, and live shows that played there featured Annie Oakley, Buffalo Bill Cody and Enrico Caruso.

NEWARK THEATRE, NEWARK. Little is found in news items concerning the Newark Theatre despite its half-century run from 1904 to 1958. In those early days, though, it was referred to as both an opera house and a playhouse.

PALACE THEATRE, SEAFORD. In 1921, W. Ford Breeding opened the third theater in Seaford's history as the New Theatre at the corner of High and Market Streets. Ownership would eventually change to Thomas Ayers, and the name would change to the Palace Theatre. In 1935, it burned down but was rebuilt by Ayers the following year, keeping its name. Playing August 31, 1939: First National Pictures' comedy *Sweepstakes Winner.*

PARK THEATRE, WILMINGTON. The 1,100-seat Park Theatre opened in August 1920. An early screening of note happened in 1923 with the exhibition of a film showing views of the powder mills along Delaware's Brandywine River as they existed when they were in operation. This was believed to have been the only motion picture in existence to depict the oldest powder manufacturing plant in the world. Playing August 31, 1939: *Daughters Courageous*, starring John Garfield, Claude Rains and the Lane Sisters.

THE PLAYHOUSE, WILMINGTON. Delaware's fourth-oldest theater still in existence (as of this writing) broke ground just three months after the Hotel DuPont opened, and in just 150 working days, the Playhouse was complete (1913). The theater screened its first motion picture one month after it opened on a device called the Magnaphone, an invention of Wilmington native George R. Webb. By 1939, The Playhouse was committed to live theater and no longer screening films. It was closed for the season on August 31 of that year.

QUEEN THEATRE, WILMINGTON. In 1916, after 127 years as a hotel, the building at Fifth and Market was converted by the Wilmington Amusement Company into a movie palace, receiving rave reviews. Playing August 31, 1939: the ninth and final installment in the Torchy Blane series of films, *Torchy Plays with Dynamite*, starring Jane Wyman as wisecracking reporter Blane.

REESE THEATRE, HARRINGTON. Like other theaters in the state's history, this one began as the town's opera house (1900) and was eventually replaced. In its early days, the Reese Opera House served the Harrington community by hosting events like dances, graduations and meetings of the Farmers Institute. Playing August 31, 1939: the Jacques Tourneur crime drama *They All Come Out* and the Gene Autry western *Home on the Prairie*.

The New Castle Opera House was located on the second floor of this building (undated). *Delaware Public Archives.*

RIALTO THEATRE, WILMINGTON. In October 1908, where once was housed the Wilmington Candy Company, the Lyric Theatre opened. It would burn to the ground, be rebuilt and change owners, but eventually it settled into its best-known name, the Rialto, in 1919, and kept that name for decades to come. The Rialto Theatre was temporarily closed on August 31, 1939.

RINGLER'S THEATRE, BETHANY. Built on the beach in 1923, Ringler's Theatre was used heavily for community purposes, but it was also a fully functioning movie theater. In September 1944, a deadly hurricane landed in Delaware and leveled the Bethany boardwalk, destroying Ringler's. For all the closures of all the theaters in all the years, Ringler's appears to be the only theater in Delaware to have perished by natural disaster.

ROBIN HOOD THEATRE, WILMINGTON. Founded in 1931 and known for its live theater offerings, the Robin Hood Theatre makes this list because it was an active live theater during World War II that would eventually show movies, albeit not until the 1960s. Playing August 31, 1939: a live performance of *Kiss the Boys Goodbye*, a comedic play inspired by the search for the right actress to play Scarlett O'Hara in *Gone with the Wind*.

THE ROXY, SMYRNA. Smyrna's Roxy began first as the Smyrna Opera House in 1870, not long after the Middletown Opera House opened. And like Middletown's opera house, Smyrna's was part of the town hall, and it hosted a wide variety of events, lasting for over fifty years before temporarily closing. After a five-year run as the Como Theatre in the mid-1930s, it became the Roxy. Playing August 31, 1939: the crime picture *Waterfront*, starring Dennis Morgan and Ward Bond.

THE SAVOY, WILMINGTON. In June 1906, Wilmington had its second five-cent theater, the Moving Picture Place. (The first nickelodeon was the Comedy Theatre, which opened earlier that same year.) Over the next two years, the theater would change names three times, settling into the Savoy, a name it would keep for more than forty years. Playing August 31, 1939: Shirley Temple and Randolph Scott in *Susannah of the Mounties*.

SCHINE'S NEW PLAZA THEATRE, MILFORD. In April 1939, before Schine Chain Theatres Inc., the largest independent theater circuit in the country at the time, took over Milford's New Plaza Theatre, the (just) Plaza Theatre hosted a pair of special visitors early in its life. In November 1922, the year it opened, Assistant Secretary of the Navy Theodore Roosevelt Jr. spoke on behalf of the Republican Party, while in June 1923, President Warren G. Harding and his entourage visited Delaware as part of a trip that began in Wilmington but had a lengthy stop in Milford where, at the Plaza, the president was initiated into the Order of the Tall Cedars of Lebanon (a

This undated photo shows a haunting Ringler's Theatre on the distant, quiet boards of Bethany Beach. Before the war came to an end, the theater was destroyed in a 1944 hurricane. *Courtesy of the Town of Bethany Beach Cultural and Historical Affairs.*

The Robin Hood Theatre, Wilmington (circa 1941). *Delaware Public Archives.*

side degree of Freemasonry). Playing August 31, 1939: the B-drama *Career* and James Whale's *The Man in the Iron Mask* starring Joan Bennett, Warren William and Alan Hale.

State Theatre, Newark. Half a century before the State became a rep house legend (with all those midnight screenings of *The Rocky Horror Picture Show*), Louis Handloff opened the seven-hundred-seat theater in 1929.

The Strand, Wilmington. Not to be confused with Smyrna's Strand Theatre, Wilmington's Strand, when it opened in 1920, featured music furnished by a full string orchestra, and the lighting in the theater changed color with each picture shown. Playing August 31, 1939: Barbara Stanwyck in the railroad western *Union Pacific*.

Strand Theatre, Smyrna. Not to be confused with Wilmington's Strand, Smyrna's Strand Theatre began around 1921 as the Horace David–built Palace Theatre (not to be confused with Milford's Palace Theatre). Two years later, Mark McManus bought the place and changed the name to the Strand Theatre. In 1927, the theater changed hands again when it was bought by Kent County film exhibitor George Schwartz, owner of Dover's Temple Theatre and Opera House. Playing August 31, 1939: the Irving Berlin musical *Second Fiddle*.

Sussex Theatre | Ayers Theatre, Georgetown. Before Sussex County exhibitor Thomas Ayers turned this into the Sussex Theatre in 1931, it came to life as the Peoples Theatre in 1912 and then Ryons Theatre in 1920. It fell victim to a blaze in spring of 1941 and was rebuilt by November with a new name, the Ayers Theatre. Playing August 31, 1939: *The Rookie Cop* (starring Ace, the Wonder Dog) and *Daughters Courageous*.

Temple Theatre, Dover. A place called Boyd's Theatre in Dover burned down in 1916, leaving the state capital with only one entertainment venue, the Dover Opera House. A year later, George Schwartz opened the Temple Theatre, the first in what would be many he and his family would own over the decades.

Waller Theatre | New Waller Theatre, Laurel. In 1913, T.J. Waller built the Waller Theatre. Like many theaters in Delaware's history, this one burned down (1922), was rebuilt and reopened (1923), then burned down and was rebuilt again (1940–41). Playing August 31, 1939: *Good Girls Go to Paris* with Joan Blondell and Melvyn Douglas, and *6,000 Enemies* with Walter Pidgeon.

Warner Theatre, Wilmington. See "The History: From Opera Houses to Movie Palaces in the First State (1868 to 1939)" for detailed information about the Warner Theatre's beginnings just months before the start of World War II. Playing August 31, 1939: *When Tomorrow Comes*, with Charles Boyer and Irene Dunne.

This is Newark's State Theatre as it looked in 1954. The film on the marquee, *A Guy with a Grin*, is a re-release of the film *No Time for Comedy*, which debuted at Wilmington's Warner Theatre in September 1940. *Photo by Leo Laskaris; Newark Historical Society.*

The Temple Theatre, Dover (circa 1946). *Delaware Public Archives.*

In addition to those forty theaters, the following eight theaters opened in Delaware during World War II.

Avenue Theatre, Rehoboth. The Derrickson family—patriarch William, his son Richard and Richard's daughter Tiffany—has been the dominant film exhibition force in Sussex County, owning (in total and across time) a dozen theaters, and it all started in June 1941 with the opening of Rehoboth's Avenue Theatre, which, when it began, was open only at night (unless daytime rain hit the beach resort).

Crest Theatre, Wilmington. The state's 101st theater overall opened in style with a private party the night before offering the public Alfred Hitchcock's *Suspicion*.

Delmar Drive-In (1), Delmar. Opening in 1941, the first Delmar Drive-In (there were two in the town's history) seems to have had no formal name beyond things found in ads like "Drive-In Theatre," "Open Air Movies," "Drive-In Movies," etc. Regardless, the theater holds the distinction of being Delaware's first drive-in theater, predating Delaware's formal drive-in era, which began in 1949 with the opening of the Brandywine Drive-In (which has long been considered Delaware's first drive-in—but no).

This 1944 poster warning against the spread of malaria via mosquitos may have hung somewhere at the Delmar Drive-In (1) during the war. *National Archives and Records Administration.*

The Theater at the Dover Air Base (August 29, 1943). The double feature that day was *Here Comes Kelly* and *Honeymoon Lodge*. *Delaware Public Archives.*

THE THEATER AT DOVER ARMY AIR BASE/DOVER ARMY AIR FIELD, DOVER. The history of what is now known as the Dover Air Force Base begins in 1940, with the base really springing to action after the bombing of Pearl Harbor. Not long after that, a movie theater, which doubled as a chapel, was added. The slight name change took place in 1944.

EDGE MOOR THEATRE, WILMINGTON. Less than two weeks before Pearl Harbor—on November 26, 1941—and one day after an invitation-only private screening of *It Started with Eve*, the three-story Edge Moor Theatre opened to the public. The theater was one part of a larger shopping and residential complex that included a department store, restaurant, apartments and shops.

THE THEATER AT FORT MILES, LEWES. Another military base theater in Delaware's history was at the south end of the state. While Fort Miles itself was established in 1941, its three-hundred-seat theater opened in March 1942.

LAYTON THEATRE, SEAFORD. In 1941, twenty years after Seaford's Palace Theatre came into existence, owner Thomas Ayers opened the Layton Theatre, named after his son.

THE THEATER AT NEW CASTLE ARMY AIR BASE, NEW CASTLE. The other on-base theater to open around the same time as Dover Army Air Base and Fort Miles was housed in New Castle, although its existence came to an end not long after the end of the war.

THE SHORT BEFORE THE FEATURE

Theaters Help Between Poland and Pearl Harbor

A great amount of help was given to a great number of people during America's involvement in World War II. But that assistance—to neighborhoods, towns, cities, the state, our country and other countries—didn't start on December 7, 1941; it started well before that. We are a helpful and generous community and nation, and we always have been, whether in peace, at war or that odd place in between.

Polish War Relief

After Germany invaded Poland to start World War II, former U.S. president Herbert Hoover organized the Commission for Polish Relief (CPR), a national organization to raise money for food and supplies to help the citizens of Poland. To kick things off locally, the Polish Relief Committee of Wilmington, formed by the Council of Polish Societies of Delaware, hosted a mass meeting at the Ace Theatre to tell of the plight the Poles were suffering. The thousands of dollars that would be raised between that night and the end of 1941 (the program stopped when America joined the war) were either sent directly to Poland via the Red Cross or used to buy clothing and blankets to be shipped there.

British War Relief

Also near the start of World War II was born the British War Relief Society of America (BWRS), another organization created to aid victims in war-torn countries. Like the Commission for Polish Relief, the BWRS collected money and supplies to send overseas to those in need.

Theatrical involvement for BWRS fundraising seemed scant, at least before Pearl Harbor. In April 1941, the Defense Committee of the Women's College, University of Delaware, hosted two BWRS screenings of *Pot o' Gold*, starring Jimmy Stewart and Paulette Goddard, at Newark's State Theatre. A newsreel and the cartoon *Fishing Made Easy* played before the feature.

In June 1941, a screening was held not at a theater, but at the Soda House on the estate of R.R.M. Carpenter, who at the time was the chairman of the Delaware Chapter of the American Red Cross, but who had previously been an executive at the E.I. du Pont de Nemours Company, where he was influential in transforming the corporation from an explosives manufacturer to a diversified chemical company. He would later go on to become a majority stakeholder of the Philadelphia Phillies.

The Soda House had originally been used in making powder, but Carpenter remodeled it and included within it a functioning screening room where he would host friends for private film screenings (sometimes before those films were released to the public, to give you a sense of how influential he was). The June 1941 screening was open to the public and was held specifically to benefit the families of the Royal Air Force. It was a double feature of *Thumbs Up*, a collection of shorter films spotlighting the evacuation of Dunkirk, along with newsreel images of the war, and *The World on Fire*, a collection of newsreels showing the events leading up to the war. The latter film was edited together by Carpenter himself.

Finnish War Relief

In November 1939, Russia invaded Finland for strategic purposes, and although the Finns put up a good fight, Russia's sheer numbers were too much for them; the Finns ceded to Russia's demands in March 1940. But during those four months, Delaware did its part to try to help the Nordic underdog.

The Finnish Relief Fund was a national fundraising effort instituted by former U.S. president Herbert Hoover to help noncombatant Finns impacted by the Russian invasion. In January 1940, as one part of Hoover's effort, motion picture exhibitors representing ten thousand theaters nationwide pledged their support. Wilmington theaters joined the effort, but rather than participate en masse on the designated days of February 16 and 17, the theaters instead split the load and spread it over four days, with the city's independent theaters taking February 14 and 15 and the Warner-owned theaters taking February 16 and 17. Nine of the city's twelve theaters participated in "Help Finland Days."

Those "Help Finland Days" had a prologue of sorts with an early promotional effort on January 26, when radio station WILM broadcast its weekly *Lobby Hobby* radio program from the Warner Theatre, dedicating that day's broadcast to touting the Finnish Relief program. Three weeks later, independent theaters Ace, Park, Rialto and Strand, along with the Warner-owned Aldine, Grand, Queen, Savoy and Warner theaters, screened documentary shorts about Finland before their features and solicited donations from patrons in their lobbies, eventually helping the City of Wilmington raise close to $30,000, which was added to the national campaign coffers exceeding $3 million. These are the films that played during "Help Finland Days":

FEBRUARY 14

Ace Theatre	*Nurse Edith Cavell*
Park Theatre	*Four Wives*
Rialto Theatre	*Little Old New York*
The Strand	*Housekeeper's Daughter*

FEBRUARY 15

Ace Theatre	*The Phantom Strikes* and *Heroes in Blue*
Park Theatre	*Four Wives*
Rialto Theatre	*Little Old New York*
The Strand	*Housekeeper's Daughter*

FEBRUARY 16

The Aldine	Louis v. Godoy Fight Pictures and *Music in My Heart*
Grand Theatre	*Santa Fe Marshal*
Queen Theatre	*Swanee River*
The Savoy	*Drums Along the Mohawk*
Warner Theatre	*The Republic of Finland* (A *March of Time* Newsreel) and *I Take This Woman*

February 17

The Aldine	*Geronimo*
Grand Theatre	*Santa Fe Marshal*
Queen Theatre	*Destry Rides Again*
The Savoy	*Drums Along the Mohawk*
Warner Theatre	*The Republic of Finland* (A *March of Time* Newsreel) and *I Take This Woman*

As for the city's other three theaters, the National was not mentioned in news items in the context of relief assistance, the Arcadia was temporarily closed and Loew's was screening *Gone with the Wind* and was forced to adhere to a strict screening schedule.

One other Wilmington location of note that participated in Finnish Relief was the Auditorium, a place that once showed movies, but during this part of its history, it was providing other live entertainment, including a five-match wrestling card on February 5 specifically for Finnish Relief. The main event was for the coveted role of wrestling's "Public Enemy #1." In one corner was Cleveland's Joe "The Dynamiter" Cox. In the other corner was current title-holder Emil Dusek from Omaha. Cox won the match, and the affair was noted as the first sporting event in the city held specifically for the Finnish Relief Fund.

Greek War Relief

In October 1940, Italy attacked Greece. Soon after, the Greek American community formed the Greek War Relief Association—an organization looking to raise money for their war-torn homeland. Where the United States went, Delaware followed, and where Delaware went, its theaters were there.

On Thursday, March 27, 1941, in agreement with all city theater managers the week prior, the Aldine held a screening of the short *Greece Fights Back* and the feature *Footlight Fever*. Tickets for the special 11:15 late-night screening were available at all city theaters and other select retailers. All proceeds would go toward the Greek War Relief Fund, with the government waiving the usual tax and with theater personnel donating their time.

In addition to the screening, the city's twelve theaters had booths in their lobbies manned by members of Philoptohos, a Greek women's organization. (Some of the women wore traditional Greek costumes when on booth duty.) Wilmington mayor Albert James, who bought the first ticket to the screening, declared the week Greek War Relief Week, which happened to coincide with the anniversary of Greece's 1821 independence. Nearly one thousand people attended the screening, and almost $2,000 was raised between ticket sales and booth collections.

Local Organizational Support

While supporting the global community through various relief efforts was important, Delaware theaters did not lose sight of the needs at home, and theaters did their part to help their communities by allowing various organizations to use theaters to collect money and items for a cause, rally support behind a cause or simply host large numbers of people who needed a place to convene to discuss their cause. And of course, a lot of those involved screenings.

Theaters were friends of first responders. Between Poland and Pearl Harbor, the Milton Theatre hosted the kickoff for the eleventh annual Delmarva Firemen's Association Convention; the Strand (Smyrna) played host to a two-day convention of the Delaware Volunteer Firemen's Association; the Ball Theatre provided two nights of film screenings for a Millsboro Firemen's Auxiliary benefit, with local talent providing live entertainment between films each night; and the Everett hosted the Delaware Volunteer Firemen's Association just one year after its Smyrna sister, the Strand, did the same. That convention at the Everett is particularly interesting because the firemen attending were shown "confidential" films of air raids over London and the communications systems used in those raids. Those films had been shown to other first responders earlier that week at the Wilmington Library. Following each Everett screening, the army gave a lecture and an outdoor demonstration on the use of incendiary bombs.

Continuing with the theme of caring for people who care for others, the town of Lewes convened in the Auditorium there for a mass meeting to discuss plans for the Red Cross Emergency War Relief Fund. Lewes Auditorium owner Charles Horn also donated a portion of his Blue Hen Theatre building to the Delaware Chapter of the Red Cross in Rehoboth to be used to distribute sewing and knitting supplies and to make surgical dressings for the army and navy. Meanwhile in Wilmington, Loew's hosted a group of Red Cross volunteers in March 1940; their film was *Strange Cargo* starring Clark Gable and Joan Crawford. And in one non–Red Cross event, the Sussex Theatre hosted two benefit screenings for the Sussex County Chapter of the National Foundation for Infantile Paralysis.

Children's safety was a concern for some groups, and theaters helped there too, like when the State Theatre hosted about 150 child members of the Newark Bicycle Club for a safety rally. Speakers there included the president of the Delaware Safety Council, Newark's police chief and the chairman of the Lions Club safety committee. At the Ace, the Delaware Safety Council held its eighth annual Children's Safety Rally. On the docket were speakers, cartoons and shorts, plus three safety films: *On Two Wheels*, *Safety Patrol* and *Champions on Parade*.

Theaters helped women's groups as well. Back at the State Theatre, the Business Women's Club of Newark sponsored a benefit screening of *Four Mothers*, and the Cooch's Bridge Chapter of the Daughters of the American Revolution had a benefit screening of *Cheers for Miss Bishop*.

One final example of theaters working with community partners comes in the area of religion. At Claymont's Don Theatre, clergymen and nuns were invited to a screening of *Crown of Thorns*, a film about the Passion of Christ. No other information about the film is mentioned in the news item, but I suspect it was the 1923 German silent picture originally titled *INRI*. And in Kent County, at Dover's Temple Theatre, the Jewish Federation of Delaware sponsored a meeting to discuss the Seventh Annual United Jewish Campaign. Organization representatives from all over the state attended the gathering, which featured a screening of the 1941 film *A Tale of Two Worlds*, something of a promotional film produced by the American Jewish Joint Distribution Committee (JDC) showcasing the group's refugee efforts in Europe.

Local Military Support

It's easy to think of the military in the national sense when dealing with the topic of World War II, but so much support is required at home to make that happen, and theaters were in the thick of that support before Pearl Harbor.

In February 1940, Fort DuPont hosted a screening of *Mr. Smith Goes to Washington* to raise money for the Army Relief Society, an organization "responsible for rendering financial assistance to widows and orphans of Regular Army personnel."* A month later, the base theater hosted a guest speaker to explain what the society does.

* *Army: Magazine of the Association of the United States Army* 10, no. 1.

In mid-September 1940, several theaters hosted going-away events for guardsmen and their families before the "citizen soldiers" shipped off to basic training, including the New Plaza, Capitol, State and Warner theaters. The Warner party involved 1,200 men and their guests and included the screening of the film *Hired Wife*; at the Capitol, guardsmen in uniform could see free movies any Tuesday or Wednesday before shipping out.

The following month, an event less celebratory but no less important took place at the National Theatre: a mass meeting sponsored by the Wilmington Branch of the NAACP. At that meeting, resolutions were adopted condemning the government's policy of segregation in the armed forces. The resolutions were read by attorney Louis L. Redding.

In February 1941, before the men of the 261st Coast Artillery (National Guard) departed for Fort DuPont for a year's training, a going-away party was held at the Sussex Theatre. Men from Georgetown, Lewes, Rehoboth and Millsboro represented their hometowns.

That same month, the Independent Motion Picture Theater Operators of Delaware and the Eastern Shore of Maryland met in Harrington and pledged to cooperate with national defense efforts. The general purpose of the organization, which was originally formed in 1933, was to have a group to discuss and address the problems concerning the movie theater business. It was founded by Park Theatre manager A.J. DeFiore and included representation from theaters in Dover, Harrington, Newark, Rehoboth, Seaford and Smyrna.

In July 1941, Wilmington's Warner-owned theaters—the Aldine, Arcadia, Queen, Savoy and flagship Warner—announced a reduction in ticket prices, by as much as 60 percent, for soldiers, sailors and marines in uniform. Soon after, Loew's followed suit.

In New Castle, motion pictures of navy activity were screened at the New Castle Opera House for over three hundred men and boys. The event was sponsored by St. John's Lodge No. 2, AF&AM.

And in something of a film- and military-adjacent happening, the Wilmington Better Films Council convened for its fourteenth year. The group was part of a national organization whose primary interest was ensuring (morally) better films were made available to the public, as well as addressing larger issues, including an opposition to block booking and an interest in film- and theater-related legislation. At the 1941 opening luncheon, the group focused on motion pictures in national defense.

Feeding the Hungry

Less than two months after the bombing of Pearl Harbor, President Roosevelt signed into law the Emergency Price Control Act, which ultimately led to the rationing of food. But prior to that, during the war but before America's involvement in it, theaters were vital in helping collect food donations for their communities' needy.

Happening predominantly around the Thanksgiving and Christmas holidays, theaters including the Earle, Palace, State, Roxy, Delmar and Grand partnered with local schools, Scout troops, American Legion posts and other organizations to provide a variety of foodstuffs, but especially canned goods, to those in need. Theatergoers' generosity was rewarded with free movies.

Kids and Christmas

Nothing goes together quite like kids and Christmas, and for all the great contributions theaters made to their communities in the run-up to America's direct involvement in World War II, taking care of kids at Christmas is certainly at or near the top of that list.

Some events were simply opportunities for kids to see a movie, like in 1939, when the mayor of Wilmington arranged a free screening for kids at the Rialto; he also arranged another free screening at all theaters in the city for needy kids. That same year, Fort DuPont continued its annual tradition of giving kids under fifteen a visit with Santa, along with presents and candy and movies on Christmas Day in the post theater; the National Theatre hosted the Walnut Street YMCA Pioneer Clubs for a free Christmas screening. And then there was Christmas Eve Day 1940, when all twelve Wilmington theaters gave kids a free movie.

But it wasn't all movies for nothing and flicks for free. In most cases, theaters took care of the kids in exchange for the kids taking care of the community.

Food was a popular resource to collect. The State, Delmar, Earle and Roxy theaters worked with local organizations like the Girl Scouts, Boy Scouts, Lions Club and schools to provide kids the opportunity to see a movie for the price of one canned good—and they got out of school early to do so! The canned goods were then distributed to the local needy. These events also happened predominantly around the year-end holidays.

Just as clothing was sent to Poland for those in need, it was provided to people in Delaware who needed it as well. The Reese Theatre worked with Harrington's Community Committee to give kids the chance to donate an article of clothing for locals in need and in return see a free flick. More than five hundred kids donated in one 1940 event alone.

But perhaps the most popular events were those when kids got to see a free movie in exchange for a toy (usually something used that could be refurbished) that would find its way into the hands of an underprivileged child. Around the state, in towns and at theaters like Smyrna's Strand and Roxy, the Layton Theatre and the beach area's Auditorium and Blue Hen, events with names like "toy matinee" were popular and successful, and there is no better example of that than with Wilmington's theaters.

In November of all three years between Poland and Pearl Harbor, every theater in the city—cumulatively the Ace, Aldine, Arcadia, Grand, Loew's, Loew's Aldine, National, Park, Queen, Rialto, Ritz, Savoy, Strand and Warner—participated in the "Toy for Every Child" Drive. The goal each year was to collect fifteen thousand toys that youngsters all over the city

Two children donate toys at an unknown Wilmington theater for one of the city's "Toys for Every Child" campaigns (undated). *Delaware Public Archives.*

could simply place in the lobby of their favorite theater and walk right in to see a movie; there was no ticket exchanging at any of the theaters for this event. Those toys would then be refurbished as needed by city firemen and distributed to those in need just before Christmas. The program was so successful and so important, every public and parochial school in the city closed early that day so kids could donate toys and see a movie.

Not Kids and Christmas

Oh sure, Christmas is a great time for kids, but it's also a great time for seniors, and theaters recognized that too. Right around Christmas in 1939 and 1940, the National (both years), Rialto (1939) and Loew's (1940) offered seniors a free screening in partnership with the mayor's Christmas Committee. The seniors, all residents of area senior facilities, were treated to candy in addition to movies.

Kids and Not Christmas

And then some theaters decided to do things without a holiday as an excuse but still in the name of a good cause: education. In 1940, the Everett, Capitol, Strand, New Plaza and Reese theaters showed a free movie to kids who made honors at school.

All of the aforementioned efforts, and more like them for various causes, would continue during the war. (See "The Care Packages: Providing Comfort in a Time of Crisis," for more.)

THE DAY BEFORE THE DATE WHICH WILL LIVE IN INFAMY

Now Playing December 6, 1941

Around the state, the headlines of newspapers' final publications before the Japanese bombed Pearl Harbor ran the gamut from national interests to local fare, including theater-related items.

DelMarVa Leader, December 5, 1941
"Merchants Report That Sales Campaign Is Popular"
"Mystery Play by Seniors Next Friday"
"Fire Equipment and Water-Sewer System First on List of Municipal Improvements"

Milford Chronicle, December 5, 1941, First Edition
"Grangers Will Hold Annual State Session December 9–10"
"Xmas Dance Will Be Held December 30"
"Christmas Lights to Be Turned On Tomorrow Evening"

Newark Post, December 4, 1941
"Custodial Post Open at Local Post Office"
"D.A.R. to Convene Here on Saturday"
"Sunday Movie Vote Is Approved"

Seaford News, December 5, 1941
"This Week Around the World" [with the prescient subhead] "U.S. Is On Verge of War"
"Public Library Has Long List of Best Magazines On File"
"Council Discovers Needs of Firemen"

Smyrna Times, December 4, 1941
"Xmas Gifts for Kent Soldiers"
"Baby Contest in 2nd Period"
"Concert Tenor Well Received"

Wilmington Morning News, December 6, 1941
"Japan Wants Joint Commission to Prevent War"
"Youth Arrested in Alleged Plot to Extort $500"
"Queen Theatre to Be Modernized at $75,000 Cost"

(Wilmington) Journal–Every Evening, December 6, 1941
"150 Billions Set as Least Defense Cost"
"Woman Admits Fake as Amnesia Victim"
"Store Will Give Employees $21,675 in Defense Bonds"

Regardless of whether newspaper editors' focus was on global tensions or local concerns, the business of Saturday night moviegoing was a constant around the state. Where available, below is the list of movies that were screening the night of December 6, 1941—the night before American lives were changed forever.

Ace Theatre	*Charlie Chan in Rio* and *Fugitive Valley*
Arcadia	*The Maltese Falcon*
Ayers Theatre	*Arizona Bound* and *Hurricane Smith*
Capitol Theatre	*Belle Starr* and *The Smiling Ghost*
Delmar Drive-In	*The Roaming Cowboy*
Delmar Theatre	*Three Sons O' Guns*
Edge Moor Theatre	*Married Bachelor*
Grand Theatre	*Last of the Duanes* and *Mercy Island*
Layton Theatre	*Small Town Deb*

Loew's Aldine	*Two-Faced Woman*
National Theatre	*Gallant Sons*
New Waller Theatre	*Down Mexico Way* and *Parachute Battalion*
Palace Theatre	*Reg'lar Fellers* and *Thunder Over the Prairie*
Park Theatre	*Down Mexico Way*
The Playhouse*	*Out of This World* (a live show)
Queen Theatre	*Blues in the Night*
Reese Theatre	*Great Guns* and *We Go Fast*
Rialto Theatre	*Hot Spot*
Ritz Theatre	*Smilin' Through*
Savoy	*Belle Starr*
Schine's New Plaza	*Great Guns* and *Texas*
The Strand (Wilmington)	*Barnacle Bill* and *Bullets for O'Hara*
Strand Theatre (Smyrna)	*Small Town Deb* and *Kansas Cyclone*
Warner Theatre	*They Died with Their Boots On*

*There is one other interesting item of note concerning the Playhouse that fits best here. In late November 1941, the Playhouse offered *The Admiral Had a Wife*, directed by José Ferrer. The play was in town as part of a series of East Coast tune-up performances before heading to Broadway, where it was scheduled to open on December 8. That didn't happen—not just because of the bombing of Pearl Harbor, but because the play was a farce about "a young naval lieutenant's wife [who] connives to get her husband promoted in rank"* *set* at Pearl Harbor. The play would never open.

* *News Journal (Wilmington, DE)*, November 26, 1941.

THE RESOURCE DRIVES

Bacon Fat, Junk Jewelry and Other Household Weapons of War

Junk is the Cinderella of World War II. Scrap rubber, rags, metal, kitchen fats, and tin cans that once annoyed house holders as just so much rubbish, is now needed for the war materiel required by the nation. It took a Japanese bomb, hurtling earthward on the morning of Dec. 7 to make the country realize that neglected junk in backyards, cellars, and attics will help win the war.
—William P. Frank, reporter and columnist,
the News Journal, *September 9, 1942*

In January 1942, one month removed from Pearl Harbor, the United States launched the "Salvage for Victory" campaign, which called on all Americans at home to do their part for the war by collecting common household materials and turning in those items to be recycled for use in the war effort. The campaign would last for most of the war.

Aluminum

Prior to the Salvage for Victory campaign, the government needed aluminum, which would be recycled into planes, machine parts and anything else the military needed to defend the country. In the summer of 1941, housewives around the nation were asked to donate twenty million pounds of the stuff in any shape available—pots, pans, utensils, whatever. The Boy Scouts led the charge in Delaware by canvassing homes, which is where most of the

Left: The inclusion of the rising sun is an effective touch (undated). *National Archives and Records Administration.*

Right: This poster for scrap rubber offers perspective via numbers (1942). *National Archives and Records Administration.*

readily available metal could be found. Theaters pitched in too, offering free movie incentives to kids who brought one item to a designated matinee. This was done at George Schwartz's movie house trio of the Capitol, Everett and Strand (Smyrna) theaters. A similar offer was made by the New Waller Theatre in Laurel, and kids there responded with more than four hundred pieces. But it's the Milton Theatre that wins the prize for best aluminum matinee slogan: "Bring your old pots and pans! HELP COOK HITLER!"

RUBBER

In June 1942, with the Salvage for Victory campaign well underway, the focus turned to rubber, and theaters leveraged the strategy that worked so well for the prewar aluminum drive: scrap-for-movies events. The New Plaza offered a free movie to any kid who brought in an old tire; the Palace took any piece of rubber for admission (over one thousand pounds was collected that day); and the Warner, offering Leslie Howard, Raymond Massey and Laurence

Left: Disparaging caricatures of the enemy was effective propaganda (1942). *National Archives and Records Administration.*

Right: This 1943 poster offered housewives a chance to envision what their donated grease might do to gestapo creator Hermann Göring. *National Archives and Records Administration.*

Olivier in *The Invaders*, asked kids for rubber in any form so long as it totaled about three pounds. That Warner screening alone was one of the first of its kind in the country and netted about four thousand pounds of rubber from the one-thousand-plus children who brought everything from washing machine hose connections to car floor mats. News of the day's success inspired other theaters around the country to adopt similar programs.

Fat

In July 1942, the Salvage for Victory campaign incentivized housewives to save their kitchen fat and sell it for about a nickel per pound. Why? Simply put, fat is used in the manufacture of glycerin and glycerin is used in the manufacture of explosives—thus our government's desire to collect as much fat from America's kitchens as possible. While all the fat saved by Mrs. America was collected mostly at authorized butcher shops and the like, theaters played their part in getting the word out to save those drippings.

A great example of this was when the Layton Theatre screened Walt Disney's *Out of the Frying Pan into the Firing Line* in association with the local fat salvage campaign. Starring Minnie Mouse and Pluto (only a photo of Mickey in uniform appears, suggesting he was off fighting the war), the animated documentary short, using a combination of statistics and propaganda, speaks to Mrs. America of the importance kitchen fat can play in the war effort.

Examples of statistics provided in the short include the note that each year, 2 billion pounds of waste kitchen fats are thrown away, when all that fat could instead be used for 10 billion rapid-fire cannon shells on a belt 150,000 miles long (wrapping six times around earth). Examples of propagandic narration include lines like "Meat drippings sink axis war ships," "Waste frying fats speed depth charges on their way to crush Axis submarines," and my favorite, "Your pound of waste fat will give some boy at the front an extra clip of cartridges."

The short isn't very entertaining, but the messaging is effective.

Other Metals

The Warner was at it again in August 1942, this time collecting three pounds of scrap metal each from kids in exchange for a free flick (1940's *The Great Plane Robbery*). About one hundred children lined up with everything from old license plates to used roller skates, totaling around five hundred pounds, which was then hauled away to a local scrap yard. Over the coming months, the Earle worked with New Castle's William Penn School Student Council for a scrap drive matinee; the Crest collected two tons of scrap with a kids' double feature matinee; and the price for kids to catch a free movie at the New Plaza was ten pounds of scrap.

At the Ball Theatre, owner Huck Betts hosted a "tin can matinee," where any boy who brought a can got to see a movie for free, but there was a twist: the boy who brought the most cans would win a four-week pass to the theater. (It was reported one lad had twenty bushel baskets of cans.) The free ticket offer and weekslong pass contest were also available to girls, who were asked to bring old rags instead of cans. Also hustling for tin was the Crest, where twenty cans got a kid into a matinee.

Copper was also in demand, and the Ritz invited people of all ages to a full two-hour slate of on-screen offerings (shorts, cartoons, newsreels and the feature *The Big Stampede* starring John Wayne) in exchange for copper culled from any household item—utensils, wire, piping, even pennies. Brass was an

Above: This replica of the Tin Man from *The Wizard of Oz* sits atop a scrap metal pile collected as part of the Salvage for Victory campaign (October 1942). *Delaware Public Archives*.

Left: Likely part of the Salvage for Victory campaign, this poster reminded people where they could find tin in household items (undated). *National Archives and Records Administration*.

In this undated photo, children participate in a scrap drive like those organized by theaters around the state during the war. *Delaware Public Archives.*

acceptable substitute, as both it and copper were needed for the production of anti-tank and anti-aircraft shells and cartridges.

The New Waller planned to get in on the act with a scrap matinee, where two pounds of copper (or brass or bronze) got you in for free. Also on the copper kick was the Warner, which offered a matinee screening of *China*, starring Loretta Young and Alan Ladd, in exchange for a half pound of copper and one cent cash (to cover the tax). There were 175 kids in attendance that day, who paid with items including wire, gaskets and even a bronze statue. New Castle got organized too, with a Civil Defense Committee scrap drive screening at the Earle; the films played were the musical comedies *Stars on Parade* and *Trocodero*.

Paper

Another hot item to recycle was paper, and theaters helped collect tons of that too, including the Earle, which again worked with William Penn School students, who collected 4,500 pounds; the theater also had a general paper screening where admission to the film was 50 pounds. At the Laurel School,

In this undated photo, Boy Scouts in Lewes participate in a paper drive like those organized by theaters around the state during the war. *Delaware Public Archives.*

there was a friendly contest to see which grade could collect the most paper. The tenth grade won by collecting 3,308 pounds, earning every member of the class passes to the New Waller. Smyrna's Strand got creative, too, setting different "costs" for admission, based on age, for its paper matinee: 10 pounds for those under twelve, otherwise 25 pounds.

Stockings

Again Uncle Sam called on the women of this country to donate another common household item to the war effort. This time it was stockings in November 1942. Any silk in those leggy donations would be used to make gunpowder bags for the army and navy, while nylon would be repurposed for things like parachutes. Theaters were mostly uninvolved in the collection of stockings; that was left to retail merchants. But there is an interesting adjacent story involving stockings and a Delaware theater.

The military's demand for nylon was so high, ladies' stockings were rare. So imagine the interest at the New Waller in December 1944 when one of the items up for bid at an auction held in the theater as part of the Sixth War Loan Drive was two pairs of nylon stockings. The winning bid was $10,000.

But not all household materials were recycled into war materiel.

Records

As in vinyl. You know, phonographs.

Around June 1942, bandleader Kay Kyser, singer Kate Smith and western legend Gene Autry, among others, recognized the importance of music to the men serving around the world. But the music industry was faced with shortages of shellac, the material used at that time to make records. (The primary sources for shellac were controlled by the Japanese.) The solution was the formation of Records for Our Fighting Men, a nonprofit created with the hopes of collecting 37.5 million record albums. The proceeds from the sale of those records would be put towards buying new records to be distributed to military bases both home and abroad, while the shellac of those old albums would be reconstituted and used to make new records with all new recordings.

In July of that year, Delaware joined the nationwide record-collecting campaign led by the American Legion. Receptacles were placed around the city and state, including at the Warner, New Plaza, Palace, Layton and Milton theaters. The American Legion even went so far as to attach hammers to barrels so that folks donating discs could release a little stress and smash that shellac. (The donations were more easily transported and managed when in pieces anyway.) The final tally was 14,592 records from Delaware, part of the 11 million collected nationally.

The summer of 1943 brought another Legion-led vinyl drive, dubbed "More Records for More Fighting Men." The campaign also had more help, as churches, Boy/Girl Scouts, Kiwanis/Rotary/Lions Clubs and the Wilmington Music Commission formally joined the effort, as did the Warner, New Plaza, Loew's Aldine and National theaters. At the close of the second campaign, approximately 10,000 records were collected in the state.

Books

Originally known as the National Defense Book Campaign, the Victory Book Campaign was born of a collaboration among the American Library Association, the American Red Cross and the USO as a joint effort to get books to soldiers and sailors serving around the globe. The campaign lasted two years (1942–43) and while Delaware's efforts were largely directed by librarians, educators and others in similar fields, theaters did their part by serving as drop-off points for people who wanted to donate books. Theaters that participated include the New Plaza, Avenue, Loew's Aldine and Palace. When the Victory Book Campaign ended at the end of 1943, a move made when the War and Navy Departments purchased thirty-five million books for servicemen, some seventeen million books had been collected nationally.

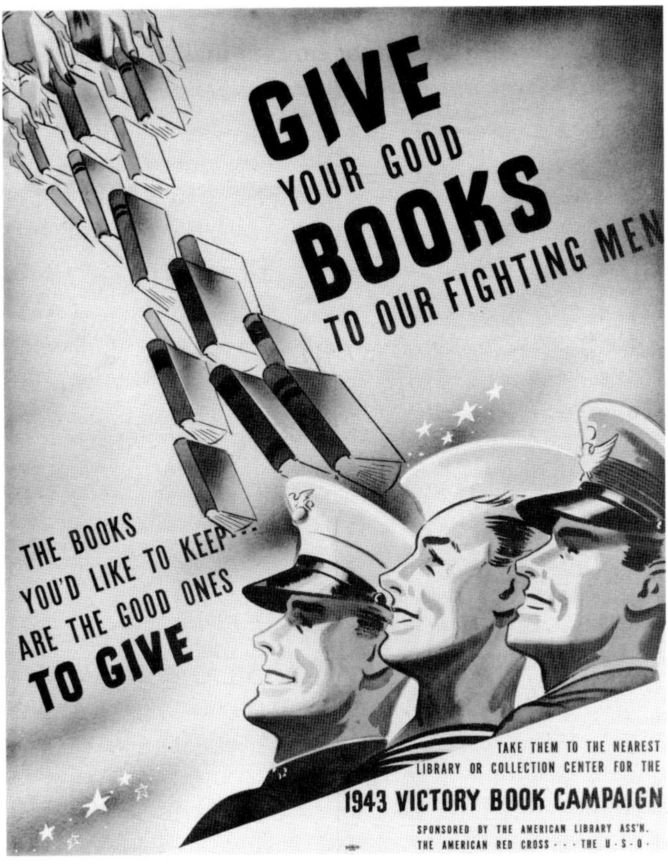

Victory Book Campaign poster (1943). *National Archives and Records Administration.*

JUNK JEWELRY

Unlike most of the other household resources that were collected and transformed into something else, junk jewelry was collected and sent as-is to men fighting in the Pacific to be used as barter with "the natives" (as news reports called them). It was told that Pacific natives would exchange services for spangly baubles. One piece of the stuff could get a soldier laundry services for a week; two pieces could net a GI five foxholes dug.

In September/October 1943, as organized by the Dover unit of the American Women's Voluntary Services (AWVS), collection points, including movie theaters, were set up around the state, and collection efforts were organized at local schools. The campaign netted 35,561 pieces of junk jewelry in Wilmington alone—more than twice that donated in the city of Los Angeles (approximately 17,000 pieces). An additional 4,262 pieces were collected around the state, including the tally of 134 pieces gathered at New Castle's Earle Theatre.

As a neat postscript, a Universal Newsreel was filmed about the drive and included many Delawareans who were key to its success.

VICTORY GARDEN

This particular resource "drive" was less about getting something to the troops and more about replenishing the homefront with what was otherwise being diverted to the troops. Victory Gardens have their roots in World War I, when America, before engaging in that war, acted to aid Europe with its war-borne food crisis by starting millions of garden plots wherever there was clear earth to grow something. It was so successful that when America found itself in the second global conflict of the century, the plan was reinstituted, this time with greater domestic stakes, as much of this country's crops were being diverted to our troops overseas, and transportation—which would normally be used to deliver food around the country—was being used by the military for troop and munitions movement. With help from educational pamphlets distributed by the government, America's "Soldiers of the Soil" once again took to Mother Earth, and by 1944 some twenty million Victory Gardens produced eight million tons of food—or about 40 percent of all fresh fruits and vegetables consumed in the country.

While theaters don't appear to have been involved directly with Victory Garden efforts, they showed propaganda films encouraging the practice,

Mrs. F. Lyman Dewey of the American Women's Voluntary Services displays some of the pieces collected in the Junk Jewelry Drive (October 9, 1943). *Delaware Public Archives.*

including the animated short *Barney Bear's Victory Garden*, which played at Loew's Aldine in 1942, and the DuPont-backed *Soldiers of the Soil*, which one news item reports to have played at the "Nemours Theater," likely a small screening room in the Nemours building.

THE BOMBSHELLS

WAACs, WAVES, WASPs and Other World War Women

It's hard to think of women in World War II and not think of Rosie the Riveter. The fictional character, whose steely gaze, curled bicep and polka-dot bandana, with the phrase "We Can Do It!" in bold type above her head, was created by artist J. Howard Miller and began as the center of a campaign to recruit women into the workforce while men were off fighting the war. Since her creation in 1942, Rosie has become something of a pop culture mainstay, emblazoned on everything from T-shirts to refrigerator magnets (this author even has a potholder with that image on it) and adapted to suit whatever cause needs some kind of rallying cry around it. But despite how critical women were to the workforce during World War II, their contributions during the era extended far beyond that, and theaters were key participants.

WAACs and WACs

The Women's Army Auxiliary Corps (WAAC) was created in May 1942 "for the purpose of making available to the national defense the knowledge, skill, and special training of women of the nation."* Their purpose was to perform noncombat army functions so that the men in the army performing those functions could instead be deployed to fight the war. Some responsibilities

* Official Home Page of the U.S. Army, army.mil.

The author found no reference to WOWs in Delaware (nearby Aberdeen, Maryland, had them at the Proving Ground) but rather likes this poster, particularly how the WOW's bandana pays homage to Rosie the Riveter, but with bombs instead of polka dots (1943). *National Archives and Records Administration.*

WAACs assumed were basic functions like clerical work but also more skilled assignments such as radio operations and air traffic control. WAACs also ran post theaters. When the program began, over thirty-five thousand women applied for fewer than one thousand positions. Of the approximately sixty women from Delaware who applied, two made it.

But as the war continued and the calendar changed to 1943, that early excitement waned, requiring the army to aggressively increase its recruiting efforts. This is when theaters got involved.

Beginning in February 1943, non-WAAC women's groups in and around Wilmington manned WAAC recruiting booths at business locations across the city, including stations at the Loew's Aldine and the Warner. Those specific booths were manned by representatives of organizations including the Business and Professional Women's Club, the International Federation of Catholic Alumni and the YWCA.

March through June 1943 was busy for WAAC recruiting all over the state, and not just with booths. In many instances, members of the WAACs and the army also spoke directly to theatergoers before feature presentations. These efforts took place at the Ayers, Capitol, New Plaza, Warner, Ritz, Loew's Aldine, Grand, Queen, Arcadia, Savoy and Rialto theaters. WAACs even made their plea to young women at a dance hosted in the rec hall at Fort Miles.

July brought a significant change to the WAACs. Until that time, the organization's members realized only certain military benefits, as it was an auxiliary group and not a whole part of the army. On July 1, 1943, President Roosevelt signed legislation that made the WAAC a full part of the U.S. Army, which afforded the women the same privileges, benefits and ranks as the men. With that, the Women's Army Auxiliary Corps rebranded to become the Women's Army Corps (WAC).

That change also brought with it an increased need to bolster ranks, and the WAC recruiting effort in Delaware's theaters continued into the fall, with visits to the State Theatre, the Blue Hen and Avenue theaters in Rehoboth and at least one of Seaford's theaters. October came, and efforts around the state increased even more. In addition to the ongoing placement of booths in theater lobbies (booths that were now being staffed by off-duty WACs) and WAC speaker presentations, army brass appearances at theaters became more frequent; the Wilmington WAC Recruiting Committee was formed (which included several theater managers); and meetings were held between army officials and mayors from towns all over the state south of Wilmington, from Middletown to Lewes.

Left: WAAC recruiting poster (1943). *National Archives and Records Administration.*

Right: WAC recruiting poster (1943). *National Archives and Records Administration.*

Theaters, already providing that lobby space and allotting time to speakers, were incentivized to do even more. In May 1944, the National Committee for the Motion Picture Industry enlisted the help of theaters and managers to participate in WAC Anniversary Week (May 11–17); the Park Theatre's A.J. DeFiore was Wilmington's representative. The national campaign offered the potential for an official army citation for each theater whose booth recruited a "squad" of twelve WACs. There was even WAC birthday cake!

WAC-specific film screenings were also part of the mix, accompanying presentations by WAC and army officials. The Warner and Queen screened *We're in the Army Now*, a WAC recruiting film (shot when they were still known as WAACs) that shows the lifecycle of a WAC, from registration to training to assignment, and the important roles WACs play in the war. The Arcadia screened *Women at War*, a dramatic short about three women who become WACs; that film would go on to be nominated for a Best Short Subject (Two-reel) Oscar.

The WACs didn't limit their recruitment screenings to theaters, however. They showed WAC films in the Ursuline Convent at a meeting of the

Wilmington Circle, International Federation of Catholic Alumnae, and they screened *To the Ladies* at the Red Cross Veterans' Bureau, where women ages twenty to fifty were invited to attend. But perhaps the most special screening of the era was in 1945, when twenty-five WAC mothers were given a personal tour of the New Castle Army Air Base where their daughters were stationed. While there, they were treated to refreshments and shown *Keep Your Powder Dry* in the base theater. The MGM drama, starring Lana Turner and Agnes Moorehead, tells the story of a group of women adjusting to WAC life.

In the end, more than 150,000 women served as WAACs and WACs, making invaluable contributions to the war effort.

WAVES

Soon after the creation of the WAAC, the U.S. Navy got on board and made WAVES: Women Accepted for Volunteer Emergency Service. The navy's intent was the same as the army's: place women in noncombat positions so that more men could serve in combat, but there were differences. Unlike the WAACs/WACs, who were first an auxiliary group before being converted in 1943, the WAVES were afforded full military status from the outset. At least one-third of the WAVES were assigned to duties related to naval aviation ranging from air traffic control to celestial navigation training to bomb trajectory calculation. In fact, the navy actively recruited college-educated women with mathematic and engineering degrees to become WAVES.

WAVES were involved in war-related events around the state during the era, but the only theater-specific connection I could find was in October 1943, when the Edge Moor Theatre played host to a service flag dedication ceremony for the sixty-two Edge Moor Gardens residents who were in the armed services. Governor Bacon spoke at that ceremony, and alongside the WAVES stood members of the WAC, representatives from the New Castle Army Air Base and Fort DuPont, the U.S. Navy, the Boy Scouts and others.

WASPs

The Women Airforce Service Pilots (WASP) program was established in August 1943 when two similar preexisting organizations merged: the Women's Auxiliary Ferry Squadron (WAFS) and the Women's Flying Training Detachment (WFTD).

WAVES recruiting poster (1944). *National Archives and Records Administration.*

The WAFS was the older of the two groups, and its origin begins in Delaware, at the New Castle Army Air Base, in September 1942. Led by Nancy Harkness Love, the War Department–created, NCAAB-headquartered squadron began with six (of an eventual forty) experienced women pilots whose task it was to deliver planes from manufacturers to military bases across the country. Like many other roles during wartime, the broader purpose of using women for this specific duty was to free men to serve overseas.

On the local movie front, there were two items of note. In September 1942, the Warner held a private screening of *Wings and the Woman* for local WAFS and other NCAAB officers. The film is a biopic about British pilot Amy Johnson, the first woman to fly from England to Australia, who went missing in January 1941 while on a ferrying mission not unlike those carried out by the WAFS. In October 1942 it was reported that producer Walter Wanger received permission to shoot scenes at the NCAAB for an upcoming film about the squadron; the title at the time was *The WAFS.* That film was eventually completed, it was renamed *Ladies Courageous* (starring Loretta Young) and it was released in June 1944. It first screened locally at the Queen.

The WFTD was established by Jacqueline Cochran in Houston, Texas, in November 1942. In addition to ferrying aircraft like the WAFS, the WFTD tested aircraft for repair needs, transported targets for anti-aircraft practice and flew searchlight tracking missions.

In August 1943, the two groups merged and became WASPs; Cochran was the director of the organization and its training division, with Love assuming ferrying division director duties. While there doesn't appear to be any direct connection during the World War II era in Delaware, WASPs and theaters participated in the same war bond campaigns, and since other women's groups such as the WAACs and WACs partnered directly with theaters, it's possible WASPs did the same. It's also likely local theaters screened short subjects or newsreels about the organization. The unit was disbanded by the army in December 1944.

SPARs

Just as the army had WACs and the navy had WAVES, so too did the Coast Guard have its own all-woman division to staff noncombat roles normally held by men. In November 1942, the SPARs were born. The acronym was

SPARs recruiting poster (undated). *National Archives and Records Administration.*

taken from the Coast Guard's motto, which is "Semper Paratus," meaning "Always Ready." Semper Paratus, Always Ready. SPAR.

In August 1944, the Rialto Theatre screened *Battle Stations*, a short documentary about the origins of the SPARs, and in October 1945, Marjorie Grenier, a SPAR stationed in Bethany Beach, joined the traditionally male-only Fort Miles Players in the live musical revue *One Touch of Genius*. (See "The Entertainment: Putting on a Show Over Here Before Shipping Off Over There," for more on the Fort Miles Players.)

The SPARs were demobilized in June 1946.

AWVS

In 1939, having been inspired by similar services she witnessed in England and abroad, socialite Alice Throckmorton McLean recruited friends to participate in a series of voluntary social services. The following year, she formally founded the American Women's Voluntary Services, and by December 7, 1941, her organization had already grown to eighteen thousand members. During the war, those numbers grew even more, as women across the country were eager to contribute to the war effort but perhaps were unable to join organizations like the WAACs or WAVES. The services the AWVS provided cannot be overstated and ranged from sewing to cryptography. On top of that, the organization sold over $1 billion worth of bonds and stamps during the war.

In Delaware, the AWVS worked with theaters on numerous efforts, not the least of which was recruiting. In July 1942, a trailer was shown in Wilmington throughout the day at the Loew's Aldine, Warner, Queen and Rialto theaters looking for volunteers to join the Delaware ranks of the AWVS, and a booth was set up in each theater where women could register. The AWVS helped other organizations recruit, too. In the latter half of 1943, some of those same city theaters screened *Glamour Girls of 1943*, a documentary short film about the importance of women workers in America's defense plants. Working in those plants might not have been part of what the AWVS did, but handing out pamphlets after the movie, on behalf of the War Activities Committee and the War Manpower Commission, to women who were interested in war work, certainly was.

In addition to contributing to that $1 billion in bond and stamp sales, local AWVS members also participated in resource drives, including collections of silk and nylon hosiery and junk jewelry, the latter of which was collected at the Earle. (See "The Resource Drives: Bacon Fat, Junk

This war bond banner appears to show the shadow of a Revolutionary War soldier behind a woman ready to support the World War II effort (circa 1942). *National Archives and Records Administration.*

Jewelry, and Other Household Weapons of War," for more information on junk jewelry collection.)

When not aiding in the war effort, the AWVS was helping communities, like the time in January 1943 when the organization conducted a voluntary fingerprint cataloguing service for use in the event of an air raid; it was conducted at the National Theatre.

And if the AWVS couldn't get to a theater, a theater got to them, as was the case in the summer of 1943, when the Ace Theatre sent its "Flying Squadron" to assist the AWVS at a street dance/bond rally in front of Wilmington's Public Building.

By the time the war had ended, the AWVS ranks had risen to 325,000 women.

Minute Maids

Not to be confused with the Minute Maids formed by the Girl Scouts in partnership with the U.S. Treasury Department during the same era, these Minute Maids were formed in 1942 as part of the growing contingent of women doing their part for the war effort. Consisting of sixteen girls from Wilmington High School—all too young to join the WAACS or WAVES, but all ready to do their part—the Minute Maids, wearing uniforms of their own design (dubbed "Victory costumes"), made their public debut on November 4, 1942, at the Hob Tea Room. The occasion was a luncheon meeting of Wilmington-area women who were working on "Women at War Week" plans. The Minute Maids' ongoing part in the war effort would be to aid in the sale of war bonds,

Invoking Pearl Harbor was effective on posters (undated). *National Archives and Records Administration.*

stamps and stamp corsages and other patriotic items at events around the city, including movie theaters.

One of those theatrical appearances by the Minute Maids occurred on December 7, 1942: "Avenge Pearl Harbor on Delaware Day," which brought with it aggressive war bond sales goals. In Wilmington theaters, guest speakers made pitches for war bonds in between films and special trailers and shorts. The Minute Maids were on hand to go through the audience to sell stamps and accept pledges for bond sales, all after canvassing houses in select areas earlier that day. In that one night, the Minute Maids helped Wilmington theaters sell $37,000 in bonds and stamps. The theaters' trailers and shorts campaign would continue through the week.

In December that same year, the Minute Maids spent a week at the National Theatre and other places in Wilmington's Black community to keep those stamp and bond sales going.

WOMEN AT WAR WEEK

In September 1942, Helen P. Gans, eastern regional advisor of the Women's Division of the U.S. War Savings Staff, advised the New Castle County Committee of the state women's division that November 22–28 would be observed as (what would eventually be named) "Women at War Week," a national program when women "will be encouraged to use their own ingenuity in dramatizing the need for war bond sales."* Delaware retailers and merchants, schools, and clubs were tapped to help and were eager to participate. Events included radio programs; jeep rides; victory teas, parties, and luncheons; sales of corsages made of war stamps; window displays; and bond sale booths. Even clergymen were asked to mention the week's efforts in their sermons. Of course movie theaters were heavily involved—most notably with the Miss Victory contest.

As part of the week's events, the Women's Division of the U.S. War Savings Staff sponsored a contest to find a symbol for women doing their part for the war effort; the title was originally "Victory Queen" but was changed to "Miss Victory." Per Mrs. C.A. Grasselli, the chair of the women's section of the group, "As a tribute to their effort, we are selecting Miss Victory. Perhaps she will be a war mother, a war worker, or a sweetheart of one of the army camps." The contest began on November 10 and concluded with the end of

* *Morning News* (Wilmington, DE), September 24, 1942.

Women at War Week. This is what the *News Journal*'s editorial board had to say on November 13 about the contest:

> *The business of naming queens by popular ballot has sometimes fallen to a pretty low level but the selection of a Victory Queen which Wilmington is now making is a patriotic endeavor. As such it is worthy of general support.*
>
> *Ours incidentally will be the first Victory Queen in the United States. Figuratively speaking, her throne will be built of guns and bullets to rout the Axis forces and her coronation gown will be made of war bonds and stamps.*
>
> *To vote for the lady of your choice all you need to do is to buy war stamps and bonds at the booths provided for that purpose at all the city's moving picture theaters. It is not even required that you attend the performance inside the theater.*
>
> *This activity is part of the "Women at War Week" campaign which opens next Sunday. By taking part in it you help your government and, of course, yourself. The lucky lady who becomes the queen will be suitably rewarded.*

Voters could nominate anyone to be a Miss Victory candidate, as long as the candidate was at least eighteen years of age, a citizen of the United States, a resident of Wilmington or its suburbs and had contributed to the war effort in such capacities as WAACs or WAVES, employees of companies contracted by the government ("war work"), members of civilian defense, participants in the Red Cross and the like.

Votes were placed by way of the purchase of war bonds and stamps. Stamps counted as one vote per $0.25 increment, while bonds counted as one hundred votes per $25 increment. Those stamps and bonds could only be purchased at—ergo, votes could be cast only at—the following twelve Wilmington theaters: Ace, Arcadia, Crest, Edge Moor, Loew's Aldine, Park, Queen, Rialto, Ritz, Savoy, Strand and Warner. The winner would receive a $100 war bond, second place a $25 war bond and third place $5 in war stamps.

In the early days of voting, eighteen women were placed on the ballot. One of those women was Bellanca Aircraft employee Eleanor Dill, who not only met the criteria as a "war worker" but also embodied the spirit of the war effort by purchasing one bond per week and walking to work every day (to save on rationed gas and rubber tires).

By the end of the first week, the nominee count had reached fifty, with theater cashiers having heard numerous human interest stories about why voters were nominating the women they were nominating, including a story from one youngster who bought a stamp and nominated his mother because she was "making things to help his brother in the service."*

During the contest, it was announced that in addition to the one-hundred-dollar bond, Miss Victory would christen a new 415-foot ship being built for the Maritime Commission by Wilmington-based shipbuilder Pusey and Jones, to be completed in the spring of 1943.

Over the voting period, local newspapers published ongoing vote tallies and provided profiles of some of the women, including Justine Donovan, manager of the dozen women assigned to a bond booth at one of Wilmington's theaters; Kathryn Geanopolis, active member of Greek organizations; Jeanette Wright, junior hostess at a local USO center; and Tillie Cohen, Wilmington's first WAAC.

At the close of the contest, a total of 242,033 votes had been cast for seventy-two candidates, translating into $60,508.25 worth of war stamps (that's a little over $1 million in 2022 money). When the votes were tabulated, the winner was Margaret A. Papaleo, who received 86,523 votes (nearly 36 percent of all votes cast).

Papaleo's war support bona fides were impressive. From her earnings as an employee with department store Kennard-Pyle, she invested 10 percent in war bonds. She manned the war stamp sales booth at the Park Theatre, was a civilian defense volunteer, played hostess at multiple USO dances, worked for the Red Cross and was a member of the AWVS. She also had two brothers in the army and a third planning to join.

Tillie Cohen took a distant second place (44,646 votes), and Kathryn Geanopolis finished third (44,348). Including Papaleo's vote total, the top three vote-getters accounted for 72 percent of the vote. For the duration of the First War Loan Drive (November 30 through December 23, 1942), Papaleo made appearances at the city's participating theaters and autographed bond envelopes. When asked what any one person could do to help win the war, Papaleo responded, "Just do your best to keep from being sick or losing time or spreading illness; work full time; and invest 10 percent in war bonds."

With a response like that, it's no wonder Papaleo took home the Miss Victory crown.

Other theaters contributed to Women at War Week, too. In one traditional effort, the Everett hosted a benefit screening where a war stamp was issued with every ticket bought. In a less traditional effort, Rehoboth theater owner Charles Horn auctioned off his moustache. That is, he let the high bidder

* *Morning News* (Wilmington, DE), November 16, 1942.

Margaret Papaleo, newly crowned Miss Victory, receives a one-hundred-dollar war bond from War Savings Staff state chairman Henry T. Bush. Looking on are (*left to right*) Wilmington mayor Albert W. James; Leah Cohen, accepting the second-place reward on behalf of her sister, Tillie Cohen; and Mrs. C.A. Grasselli, chair of the women's division of the Savings Staff (December 1942). *Delaware Public Archives.*

shave off his moustache—which he had had for twenty-two years!—in a public event, a stunt that was met with great enthusiasm. Though perhaps calling it a "stunt" is unfair. Horn was trying to demonstrate how every individual could make some sort of sacrifice in the name of bond sales and the war—that if movie stars could auction autographs or kisses, anyone could do anything. The $1,700 that won shaving rights was part of the $11,704 raised in Rehoboth for this event.

Women at War Week ended just before the start of the First War Loan Drive.

THE FLOATING SQUADRON

If you were in the city of Wilmington and you needed help selling bonds at your event, but you didn't have anyone nearby who could help, you could summon the Floating Squadron, a group of Polish women based out of the Ace Theatre and working as part of the Delaware War Finance Committee. The women of the Floating Squadron worked in business during the day but dedicated their nights and weekends to selling bonds at patriotic rallies and other events where bonds were sold, bringing their own bond-issuing equipment with them—and they were good. During the Third War Loan Drive, the Floating Squadron led all Wilmington booths in sales with over $260,000 in bonds and stamps. They even had their own uniforms, described as a blue pinafore, white blouse and red hat, which they designed. Led by "Captain" Helen Delikat, their lineup (as of February 1944) was Helen Buda, Aurelia Cieniewicz, Florence Dudzinska, Helen Durka, Elizabeth Dzielak, Jeanette Falkowska, Elizabeth Jankowski, Hedy Jankowski, Alice Kempista, Clara Kowalska, Rose Kowalska, Irene Lipka, Mary Lipka, Cecelia Lukaszewska, Mary Lukasiewicz, Margie Maliszewska, Dorothy Okoniewska, Jean Osowska, Sophie Piascinska, Laura Podgorska, Elizabeth Przybysz, Helen Sarnecka, Victoria Szemelak, Elizabeth Szymanska, Gertrude Talarowska, Sabina Wierzbicka and Catherine Zeman.

Louisa d'Andelot Carpenter

Louisa d'Andelot Carpenter was many things: a DuPont heiress (her parents were R.R.M. Carpenter and Margaretta Lammot DuPont), a foxhunter, a pilot and a socialite who kept in her circle the likes of Tallulah Bankhead, Louise Brooks, Greta Garbo and Libby Holman. But during World War II, she was the manager of the Robin Hood Theatre in a part of the suburbs of Wilmington called Arden and someone who, like those movie palace managers in the big city, was fully committed when it came to supporting Delaware servicemen.

When she took over the theater in 1941, she made considerable renovations to the open-summers-only place. Most of those were improvements to the interior, but she also paid attention to the surrounding landscape and created an outdoor pavilion. The intent was to have a place for theater parties, post-play refreshments and the like, but that design would come in very handy once the United States was involved in the war.

In June 1942, when preparing for the season to open on July 1, Carpenter indicated that each week's Wednesday-through-Saturday plays would help benefit a relief organization. The first play of the season, *George Washington Slept Here*, would help benefit the Navy Relief Society. Carpenter also announced the opening of the Robin Hood Theatre Canteen, and every Sunday night, servicemen only would be treated to that week's play free of

Robin Hood Theatre manager Louisa d'Andelot Carpenter (*second from left*) with workers (circa 1941). *Delaware Public Archives.*

charge. Before the start of the season, she had already made arrangements with Fort DuPont and the USO and was in talks with the New Castle Army Air Base.

The first Sunday did not go as planned, but that was no fault of Carpenter's. The men from NCAAB got the date wrong and showed up on June 21 instead of July 5. That didn't stop Arden from delivering. Hazel Stephens, operator of the restaurant at the theater, had the owner of the local grocery store open up; bought enough deli food, hot dogs, cake, ice cream and other items to feed upward of fifty soldiers; and enlisted local housewives to prepare the food—the men were even supplied with cigarettes. Carpenter wasn't there, but she heard about it as it was happening, and while there was no play to be had, she made immediate arrangements with a friend at one of Wilmington's theaters for the men to see a movie instead.

And then the actual first Sunday—July 5—went very well, as the theater treated 200 soldiers and sailors to dinner and a show, with meals served by women from the Arden Civilian Defense Corps, Hazel Stephens and

Carpenter herself. The following Sunday, another group of servicemen was treated to food and *Our Town*. The count after the last show of the season was in the neighborhood of 1,500 servicemen having been treated to free meals and entertainment at the Robin Hood Theatre, all thanks to the determination and spirit of Louisa Carpenter.

Helen Tindall, Katherine Riley and Mabelle Swearer

Theaters were key participants in facilitating the rise of women in the war effort, and there is no more direct correlation of theaters and women than the three women who blazed trails in theaters' front offices.

After years of working in various capacities at Wilmington's Warner theaters, Helen Tindall had become the first woman assistant manager in the city's movie houses (at the Ritz). Suddenly, she found herself thrust into the position of running the Ritz in the absence of her manager when he became ill in 1943. Her lead management role was another first for a woman in Wilmington. During her tenure as manager, she became involved in the city theaters' March of Dimes campaigns as well as with efforts to collect toys for children at Christmas.

Katherine Riley was the city's second woman assistant theater manager (at the Savoy) after years of being a cashier. In 1943, she was elevated to manager status when her boss was on vacation. While the manager assignment may have been temporary, her ascension to that role was no less important and no less earned.

Mabelle Swearer's story is a little different. The city's third woman assistant manager was first a housewife and mother but wanted to take on a career as well, so she landed a job at the Arcadia. Hard work and keen business acumen paid off, and in late 1945, Swearer was made assistant manager under Lee Levy.

Mrs. Clem Gale

Over a two-year period that ended in December 1944, this seventy-four-year-old Wilmington wife, navy mother and merchant marine grandmother collected 12,088 tin cans for the Delaware Salvage Drive. Using a small basket on wheels and canvassing trash piles and yards for blocks around

The simplicity of this imagery—rows of cans morphing into rounds—works very well (undated). *National Archives and Records Administration.*

her home, Mrs. Gale stayed "one jump ahead of the ash men," and on Sundays she and her husband would remove the tin can tops and bottoms and flatten the cans. Their rally cry when flattening those cans was "We're stomping on Tojo!"

THE WAR LOAN DRIVES

Financing the Fight Through Film

Four. Point. One. Trillion. Dollars.

That's what World War II cost the United States as adjusted to 2015 dollars. The 1940s actuals were no less gaudy: $350.5 billion, an amount greater by more than ten times all other U.S. war costs, through World War I, combined. That money had to come from somewhere, and a big chunk of it came from everyday Americans via "war loans" to Uncle Sam in the form of bond and stamp purchases.

War loan efforts in Delaware began in January 1942, with the appointments of executives to the Delaware Defense Savings Committee. Additional personnel were added, and more committees were formed across the state, completing the infrastructure and getting the machine operable. A competitive fundraising spirit was embraced between and among committee divisions, towns around the state and plants and companies, and it paid off. Before the formal period of the "first" war loan drive began in November 1942, over $28 million in bonds had been sold in the state.

Contributing to that state total were Delaware's theaters. Beginning in late May 1942, war bonds and stamps were available for purchase at every theater in the state, affording people the opportunity to buy them at any hour of any day or night each theater was open. Permanent booths were erected inside the theaters to be staffed by theater employees; not long after, women volunteers from organizations like Beta Sigma Phi, Atlas Girls' Club and multiple clubs from the YWCA voluntarily staffed those booths as well.

In May 1942, six months before the First War Loan Drive, the Wilmington Drama League went mobile on Wilmington's Market Street in its efforts to sell war bonds. Just behind them, *Tortilla Flat* was playing at the Loew's Aldine. Also behind them, the Grand Theatre was temporarily closed. *Delaware Public Archives.*

Wilmington's Grand Theatre was something of an exception. That theater was closed for business at the time, but the booth adjacent to the sidewalk was used for bond sales to accommodate outside passersby from 9:30 a.m. to 10:00 p.m. daily. To sell bonds, each theater had to be certified as an issuing agent by the U.S. Treasury Department, and they were.

To help entice film fans to invest, Hollywood stars autographed early stamp books that could be purchased specifically by Delawareans. Those stars were Jack Benny, Errol Flynn, Alan Hale, Joan Leslie, Ida Lupino and Ann Sheridan.

Across the country and throughout Delaware, theaters' first joint "event-level" effort to promote bond sales kicked off on September 1, 1942, and was set to run all month, with a campaign called "Salute to Our Heroes." And if the patriotism of the event's name didn't get you, the emotion behind the slogan would have: "Buy a Bond to Honor Every Mother's Son in Service." In Wilmington, the event had a pre-kickoff at the Queen Theatre, where

This May 1942 photo shows F. Speer of the VFW presenting a check for $2,000 worth of war bonds to Donald Ross, War Savings Staff state administrator. The theater is not identified, but based on the date and the outside lettering just visible through the left exit, this is believed to be the Loew's Aldine. *Delaware Public Archives.*

on August 31, any child could see a free film if they presented a signed (by any adult) bond pledge. Along with the free film, each youngster received an official "Junior Commando" pin from the Treasury Department. The film was *Gangs of Chicago*, and about five hundred kids participated.

The slogan for the national Salute to Our Heroes campaign was "Make It to a Billion," thus setting the goal at $1 billion worth of bonds (in terms of maturity value). Delaware's portion of that was $2.5 million. Delaware theaters had already amassed almost 10 percent of that with $200,000 in pledges before the formal event kicked off, and on the first night, Wilmington and Dover alone combined for another $83,000 in sales and pledges. The theaters and their September 1 event kickoff films (where available) were:

Ace Theatre	*The Invaders*
Arcadia	*Mayor of 44th Street*
Capitol Theatre	*Mrs. Miniver*

Crest Theatre	*True to the Army* and *You're Telling Me*
Edge Moor Theatre	*Her Cardboard Lover* and *Pacific Blackout*
Loew's Aldine	*Somewhere I'll Find You*
National Theatre	*Larceny, Inc.*
Park Theatre	*They All Kissed the Bride*
Queen Theatre	*Tough as They Come*
Reese Theatre	*Mrs. Miniver*
Rialto Theatre	*Footlight Serenade*
Ritz Theatre	*Sergeant York*
The Roxy	*Mayor of 44th Street*
The Savoy	*The Courtship of Andy Hardy*
Schine's New Plaza	*The Bowling Alley Cat* and *Mrs. Miniver*
State Theatre	*Lady in a Jam*
The Strand (Wilmington)	*They All Kissed the Bride*
Strand Theatre (Smyrna)	*Ten Gentlemen from West Point*
Warner Theatre	*Beyond the Blue Horizon*

After the Junior Commando screening and the big kickoff night, two other marquee events took place in the state. One was Paulette Goddard's whirlwind visit to Wilmington and Dover (more information on that is available in "The Stars: Celebrity Cameos in the First State"). The other marquee moment was a one-night-only event at Wilmington's Loew's Aldine: a premiere screening of *A Yank at Eton* starring Mickey Rooney. The only way to get into that screening was to buy a bond, and the better the pledge, the better the seat. The theater raised over $50,000 that night, including the money made from the sale of a block of forty tickets (with a maturity value of $1,000). The woman who purchased them knew she could not make the event, but she bought the tickets anyway and donated them to the USO.

At the end of the Salute to Our Heroes campaign, Delaware beat its quota with more than $2.6 million, more than a quarter of which was from theaters, and the country exceeded its goal as well, selling close to $1.1 billion in bonds.

Delaware then found itself not only screening movies for the war effort but actually appearing in them as well. In October 1942, the Division of Motion Pictures and Special Events of the U.S. Treasury Department sent a film crew to the First State to make a series of short films about Delaware to be added to newsreels that played around the country. Scenes in the first film included those of DuPont's original powder plant, the Brandywine River and the DuPont Experimental Station. These "Minute Man Movies," depicting hundreds of locations and occupations, had been filmed around the country beginning in March 1942. Other Delaware filming locations scheduled included more stops in Wilmington, a Kent County fruit farm and a Sussex County poultry farm. Governor Bacon filmed a brief monologue as well, touting the state's contribution to the war effort with its chemical industry, factories, shipyards and farms, as well as bond and stamp sales.

Bonds continued to be sold by theaters, including those sold by the Newark Chapter of the Women's College Alumnae Association at the Newark Theatre, with one other large money-raising effort happening the week before that First War Loan Drive: Women at War Week, which took place November 22–28. The overall event, which celebrated women's contributions to the war, was statewide, but the centerpiece was the Wilmington-based Miss Victory contest, where one lucky gal was named the first ever Miss Victory by way of votes made with bond and stamp purchases at theaters. More details on that effort can be found in "The Bombshells: WAACs, WAVES, WASPs, and Other World War Women."

The First War Loan Drive

(November 30, 1942, through December 23, 1942)

The First War Loan Drive (which wasn't even called that at that time—there was no branding of these efforts yet) wasn't a drive in the way its sequels would become familiar, but it still raised a lot of money.

The timing of the national campaign allowed the state to leverage its celebration of Delaware Day (the date in 1787 when Delaware ratified the Constitution). The theme was "Avenge Pearl Harbor on Delaware Day," further leveraging the calendar coincidence between Delaware Day and Pearl Harbor. The slogan, however, was a little clunkier: "Delaware Was First Before, Let Us Be Out in Front Now—On to Victory. Buy War Bonds."

Delaware theaters' strategy wasn't event-based; there was no one film playing anywhere that was the focus of the fundraising. Instead, the strategy was for a massive one-night sales push at all theaters at the same time, including Minute Maids soliciting audiences in Wilmington, all Wilmington programs pausing at 9:00 p.m. for the screening of a special *Remember Pearl Harbor* trailer and speakers addressing Wilmington audiences about the importance of buying bonds. The strategy worked, as movie houses (again, with no splashy premiere or singular event) sold $37,000 worth of stamps

The combination of a soldier fighting, a lonely child, "Buy Bonds" and "Remember Pearl Harbor!" checks many emotional boxes (1944). *National Archives and Records Administration.*

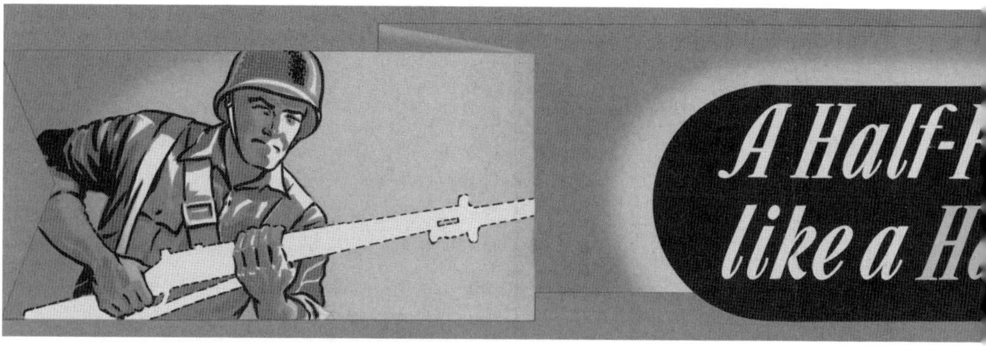

its goal was $600,000. Additionally, Loew's Inc. purchased $5 million in bonds and spread the "sales credit" among its theaters across the country; the Loew's Aldine saw $25,000 of that. And while not directly related, the Grand reopened during the drive, giving the city one more movie house where fundraising events could take place.

When the Second War Loan Drive was complete, it would be described as the greatest government financing campaign in history. The national goal was shattered: $18.5 billion was raised, some $5 billion above its goal. Delaware had similar success, raising $56.8 million against its goal of $34.7 million.

The Third War Loan Drive

(September 9, 1943, through October 2, 1943)

The Second War Loan Drive went so well, Uncle Sam postponed the Third War Loan Drive by a month, from August to September 1943. When it finally kicked off, "Back the Attack—Buy Bonds" was the rallying cry. And rally it did, but it needed to with lofty goals of $15 billion nationally and $49 million in Delaware.

President Roosevelt got things started the night before with a rousing national speech that was available on almost every radio station in the country, and theaters in Wilmington interrupted their schedules to broadcast the speech. But even before that, Wilmington was preparing, as the Drama League performed again on WDEL with a dramatic work that stressed the important role individuals play in the bond drive.

The opening morning of the Drive, the Queen Theatre hosted a mass meeting of city retailers—some 1,600 salespeople in all—who would

This banner holds civilians accountable, by way of not completing a war stamp book, for a soldier being inadequately equipped during war (1942). *National Archives and Records Administration.*

be part of the "Victory Sales Corps" to sell bonds like never before; it was requested of every salesperson to sell at least $200 in bonds during the drive. The bond film *Seven Fighting Words* was shown, and the day was capped off with a parade. Beyond the Queen playing host to the launch of the city's campaign, theaters were low-key players until later in the drive.

(Not all the retail action was happening in Wilmington. In Milford, it was announced at Armory Hall that the woman with most bond sales in the Third War Loan Drive would be crowned the "Bond Queen of Milford.")

On September 22, the Warner held a bond premiere of the musical comedy *Let's Face It*, starring Bob Hope and Betty Hutton. The price of admission was one war bond, and what made the screening particularly special was the fact the film wouldn't be released to the general public for two weeks after the bond screening, so it was a great chance for movie lovers to get the jump on a new release. (These weeks-early premieres in support of bond sales would become a staple throughout the war and its loan drives.) The premiere was a wild success, with nearly 1,800 people contributing over $1 million in one night. (About half of that was from ticket sales; the other half was from purchases for more than what was needed to secure a seat.) But theaters weren't done.

Four days later, on September 26, the Crest had a bond screening of its own, as sponsored by the Newport Civilian Defense Council, showing Lena Horne and Bill Robinson in *Stormy Weather*. The day after that, theaters across the country participated in "Free Movie Day" when, with the purchase of a bond, anyone could get into a movie for free that day. Delaware was very

much involved in that campaign, with all twelve Wilmington theaters taking part along with other theaters around the state. The theaters and their Third War Loan Drive "Free Movie Day" films (where available) were:

Ace Theatre	*Air Force*
Arcadia	*Appointment in Berlin*
Capitol Theatre	*Best Foot Forward*
Crest Theatre	*Bataan*
Grand Theatre	*They Came to Blow Up America*
Loew's Aldine	*Swing Shift Maisie*
National Theatre	*Five Graves to Cairo*
New Waller Theatre	*Stage Door Canteen*
Park Theatre	*Lady of Burlesque*
Queen Theatre	*We've Never Been Licked*
Rialto Theatre	*Claudia*
Ritz Theatre	*Bad Men of Missouri* and *Shadows of Chinatown*
The Roxy	*Ghosts on the Loose* and *Hi, Buddy*
The Savoy	*Mexicali Rose*
Schine's New Plaza	*Best Foot Forward*

Opposite: This is a promotional photo of a twenty-five-dollar war bond, reminding people that bonds are investments, not donations (1943). *Delaware Public Archives.*

Above: The specter of Nazis looms over American children (1942). *National Archives and Records Administration.*

The image of a soldier presumably burying his fellow soldiers, and perhaps not having to do so if more bonds are bought, is very effective (circa 1944). *National Archives and Records Administration.*

State Theatre	*The Palm Beach Story*
The Strand (Wilmington)	*Coney Island*
Strand Theatre (Smyrna)	*It Comes Up to Love* and *Riders of the Rio Grande*
Warner Theatre	*So Proudly We Hail*

As an added bonus, if at any time you bought a $25 bond during the first week of the drive, for an extra $1.25 you could attend a September 18 dinner at the Armory in Wilmington and rub elbows with five bona fide war heroes and three Hollywood starlets: Lynne Carver, Shirley Patterson and Annabella (just Annabella).

Carver's film career began in 1934 and included appearances in *Broadway Melody of 1940*, *Young Dr. Kildare* and the 1938 version of *A Christmas Carol* (with Reginald Owen as Scrooge). Patterson's career had only begun the year prior to her appearance in Wilmington, but it was packed with appearances in nearly a dozen films (although most were uncredited). Annabella, the artist formerly known as Suzanne Georgette Charpentier, was a French actress with over three dozen film credits to her name in both France and Hollywood. She was also known as Mrs. Tyrone Power.

At the end of the Third War Loan Drive, Delaware and the nation had done it again, with the nation collecting $19 billion against its $15 billion goal, and Delaware delivering $58 million against its quota of $49 million.

The Fourth War Loan Drive

(January 18, 1944, through February 15, 1944)

Planning for the Fourth War Loan Drive began in December 1943, before quotas at the national and state levels had even been set. Lewis Black, manager of Wilmington's Warner Theatre and city manager of all Warner-owned theaters, chaired the committee tasked with arranging the next mass meeting of retailers, set for January 18. It would again be held at the Queen Theatre.

When the quotas were set, they were lower than previous drives, though certainly still a challenge. Nationally, the goal for the Fourth War Loan Drive was set at $14 billion, with a focus on canvassing rural areas; women were also planned to be made a sales force. Delaware's quota was $43 million, with the expectation that $19 million of that would come from individual contributions. The increased focus on individuals influenced the drive's slogan—"Let's All Back the Attack"—as well as the goal that every citizen in the country buy an *extra* $100 bond.

The drive's opening day began with that retailer rally at the Queen Theatre, where Major George S. Welch was scheduled to speak. Welch was Delaware's first hero of World War II, having not only survived the attack on Pearl Harbor (where he was a lieutenant at the time) but also having had the wherewithal to scramble for an aircraft and shoot down four Japanese planes during the chaos of that December morning. That earned him the Distinguished Service Cross, a meeting with President Roosevelt, parades and more, but Welch wasn't done. A year later, while stationed in New Guinea, Welch became a bona fide ace by taking out sixteen more Japanese planes in various air skirmishes over a period of thirty-three months. Unfortunately, Welch became ill and was unable to attend the event at the Queen, but his mother took his place to rally the retailers. New Castle Army Air Base band the Jive Bombers played and everyone present was shown *December 7th*, an Oscar-winning documentary/docudrama about that fateful day in 1941, the aftermath and the ongoing efforts to beat Japan.

The day continued with a one-thousand-person-strong parade that included troops from Fort DuPont and the New Castle Army Air Base, members of the Coast Guard, WACs, SPARs, WAVES and other military and civilian groups. That night, a rally meeting at the Playhouse offered speakers, including Admiral William F. Halsey Jr., commander of the South Pacific forces, who was in the area on personal business but agreed to speak at the rally. Also part of the event were the screenings of two films: the Oscar-nominated *War Department Report*, a documentary produced by the Office of Strategic Services that uses newsreel footage and other film sources depicting things like Germany's troops and provisions, American military supply logistics and more; and *December 7th*, which had been screened at the Queen that morning.

Over the course of the Fourth War Loan Drive, theaters all over Delaware, with a self-imposed goal of selling at least one bond for every seat in every theater, were doing their part. At the start of the drive, the Capitol Theatre screened *War Department Report* and *December 7th* three days after the Playhouse, and at the end of the drive, on February 15, the Capitol held a bond premiere of *Madame Curie*, starring Greer Garson and Walter Pidgeon. Other bond premieres around Delaware included *A Guy Named Joe* (with Spencer Tracy and Irene Dunne) at the Loew's Aldine; *Sweet Rosie O'Grady* (with Betty Grable, Robert Young and Adolphe Menjou) at the State Theatre; and *Old Acquaintance* (with Bette Davis and Miriam Hopkins) at the

Left: This is a 1944 portrait of Delaware World War II hero Major George S. Welch. It is part of the Catalog of American Portraits, a research archive of the National Portrait Gallery, Smithsonian Institution. *Delaware Public Archives*.

Right: On January 18, 1944, Donald P. Ross, executive vice-chairman of the Delaware War Finance Committee, and Admiral William F. Halsey, commander of the South Pacific forces and the Third Fleet, meet before a Fourth War Loan rally at the Playhouse. *Delaware Public Archives*.

National. Other films shown around the state included another viewing of *December 7th*, this time at the Theater at Fort DuPont, and *Under Two Flags* (with Ronald Colman and Claudette Colbert), which played at both the Ayers and Layton theaters on separate nights.

There were also a pair of non-film events—one fundraising, one not—that took place at the Playhouse during the Fourth War Loan Drive. The fundraising event was a fashion show, where 30 local models sported about 150 upcoming spring styles (courtesy of Wilmington retailers Braunstein's and Bird-Speakman) to a soundtrack laid down by the Jive Bombers. That event brought in over 1,200 women and raised $200,000 in bonds (which were required for admission). The non-fundraising event invited children and their parents to learn how kids were contributing to the war effort. It was announced at that event that since the start of the war, children were responsible for generating over $1 million in stamp and bond sales. (Speaking of children, the Fourth War Loan Drive also saw the return of the Junior Commandos.)

Above: The Capitol Theatre during one of 1944's three War Loan Drive premieres. *Delaware Public Archives*.

Left: This Fourth War Loan Drive poster leverages the Third War Loan Drive's slogan, "Back the Attack" (1944). *National Archives and Records Administration*.

The last big event of the drive was another Free Movie Day, this on February 15, where every theater in the state gave a free movie ticket to every bond buyer who asked for one. The theaters and their Fourth War Loan Drive "Free Movie Day" films (where available) were:

Ace Theatre	*Thank Your Lucky Stars*
Arcadia	*Destination Tokyo*
Ayers Theatre	*Somewhere in France*
Crest Theatre	*Watch on the Rhine*
Edge Moor Theatre	*Girl Crazy*
Grand Theatre	*This Is the Army*
Layton Theatre	*Lady Takes a Chance*
Loew's Aldine	*Cry Havoc*
National Theatre	*So Proudly We Hail*
New Waller Theatre	*Thousands Cheer*
Palace Theatre	*Edge of Darkness*
Park Theatre	*The Gang's All Here*
Pike Theater	*Sahara*
Queen Theatre	*Frisco Kid*
Rialto Theatre	*Lifeboat*
Ritz Theatre	*Casablanca*
The Roxy	*The Fallen Sparrow*
The Savoy	*Manpower*
Schine's New Plaza	*Europe's Crossroads* (A *March of Time* Newsreel) and *Johnny Come Lately*
State Theatre	*The Gang's All Here*
The Strand (Wilmington)	*The Sky's the Limit*
Strand Theatre (Smyrna)	*Lassie Come Home*
Warner Theatre	*Desert Song*

Shortly before Free Movie Day, which was already on the calendar, it appeared the state was going to fall short of its quota by about $7.7 million. To prevent this failure, the state was granted permission to extend the bond-buying eligibility window to February 29, so while the drive would formally end on February 15, it would be credited with any bond sales for two weeks beyond that. It was later determined that a lag in reporting created this erroneous assessment, so the state did indeed hit its mark on time, but a final event had already been added so it went ahead as planned: a live vaudeville show, followed by a bond film premiere, at the Warner.

The vaudeville show featured a variety of entertaining acts, led by a vocal performance from Warren Covington, a native of Yeadon in Delaware County, Pennsylvania, a Coast Guardsman stationed in Philadelphia and a member of the Philadelphia Coast Guard Orchestra; he was accompanied by the Fort DuPont Continentals. Following the live entertainment was the premiere of *Riding High*, starring Dorothy Lamour and Dick Powell. The event made $500,000.

The final numbers crossed their respective finish lines at both the national and state levels, with the country landing at $16.7 billion and Delaware hitting $47.6 million.

The Fifth War Loan Drive

(June 12, 1944, through July 8, 1944)

And then they swung for the fences. Not quite four months after the official close of the Fourth War Loan Drive, the United States set the Fifth War Loan Drive goal at $16 billion—the highest amount thus far and what would be the highest of any throughout the war. Delaware's portion was $54 million. And all in less than a month.

Theaters would come up huge.

Serious planning began on May 25 when a group of theater managers convened at Mayor Edward Evans's office in Milford (he was the manager of Schine's New Plaza Theatre) to discuss a statewide "Premiere Night." The initial idea would eventually become an event where seventeen theaters across the state would screen a movie premiere on the same night: June 21. Admission would be by bond purchase only. Another meeting in Rehoboth was scheduled to take place closer to June 12 to finalize details.

An advance meeting of another kind took place at the Playhouse on June 6, which was open only to members of Loan Drive committees, household canvassers and other volunteers. It was the first time in any Loan Drive that the entirety of the state's war finance personnel were called to a meeting. The purpose was to prepare for the biggest Loan Drive to date, and to help motivate folks, speakers included Gale F. Johnson, the architect of the national bond/stamp sales force, and William B. Coyne, national field director of the War Finance Division of the Treasury. Attendees were also shown two films that were billed as "restricted War Department films": *Battle for the Marshall Islands*, which documents the military's preparations

Left: American-born opera star Vivian Della Chiesa performed for retailers at the Fifth War Loan Drive kickoff meeting at Wilmington's Queen Theatre on June 12, 1944. *Delaware Public Archives.*

Right: Delaware governor Walter Bacon sells a bond to Mrs. Catherine Montero of Wilmington to kick off the Fifth War Loan Drive. *Delaware Public Archives.*

for that battle; and *Beachhead Operation—Anzio*, which depicts the battle for that Italian beachhead.

The Queen Theatre entered the picture next to formally kick off the Drive on June 12, as once again it played host to a mass meeting of retailers, where every salesperson was asked to sell $300 worth of bonds. At this event, opera singer Vivian Della Chiesa performed. Also around that time, Governor Bacon was manning a booth at Rodney Square and selling bonds at the rate of (literally) one bond per minute. That night, there was a parade attended by twenty-three thousand people, where the governor, in his speech, said war bonds should now be referred to as "invasion bonds."

Two days later, the Playhouse was back in the spotlight as it hosted the Book and Authors Rally on June 14. This was no ordinary fundraiser; items of literary consequence would be auctioned here, with two catches: the highest bidder would buy war bonds in the amount of the winning bid, and the item won in the auction would be donated to a library or other institution (with exceptions). This was on top of the bond purchase required just to get in, and on top of any bond-related incidentals, like autographs from the authors in attendance:

- Carl Carmer, author of *Stars Fell on Alabama*
- *Wilmington Morning News* columnist Marquis W. Childs, author of *Sweden: The Middle Way*
- Bertita Harding, author of *Phantom Crown*
- Robert Lawson, illustrator of *Ferdinand the Bull*
- Pulitzer Prize winner Mark Van Doren, who was also chairman of the Book and Authors War Bond Committee

(If the name Mark Van Doren sounds familiar, you may better know the name of his son Charles Van Doren, who was involved in a scandal with the television trivia show *Twenty-One*. The elder Van Doren was played by Paul Scofield in the 1994 film about that scandal, *Quiz Show*.)

Clifton Fadiman, noted quizmaster and book reviewer, was in attendance to act as auctioneer. The items that were up for auction were amazing, and included:

- The original manuscript of Dr. Henry Seidel Canby's "Family History," which had not yet been published and included information not only on his own family, but on other notable Delaware families like the Tatnalls, the Shipleys and the Prices
- An original illustration by N.C. Wyeth titled *Robin Hood and Little John* as found in the *Anthology of Children's Literature*
- Eight autographed letters from authors Thomas Wolfe, Carl Sandburg, Sinclair Lewis and others
- A limited edition copy of the book *The Dutch and Swedes of Delaware*, written by Christopher Ward and illustrated by N.C. Wyeth (it was copy no. 1 of one hundred and came with a page of the original manuscript)

The highest bids were made by corporations at $1 million each. The Wyeth painting was purchased by the Continental American Life Insurance Company and was donated to the University of Delaware, while the Canby manuscript was donated to the Historical Society of Delaware by the Coca-Cola Company.

The final numbers were quite something. The 1,200-person attendance cost brought in $1.6 million in bonds. The rest of the money—from tickets to

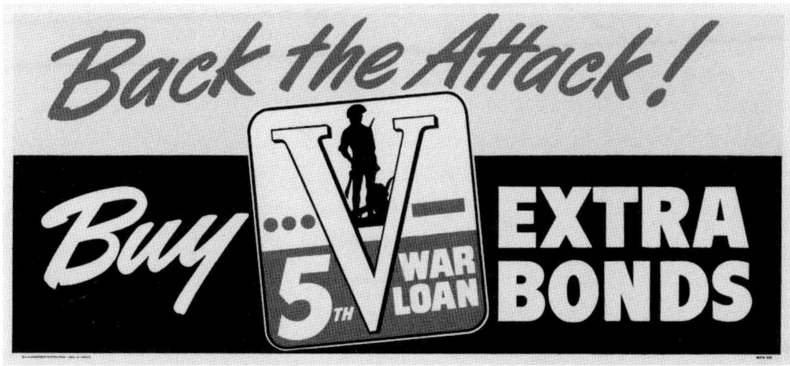

This Fifth War Loan Drive poster leverages the Third War Loan Drive's slogan, "Back the Attack" (1944). *National Archives and Records Administration.*

dine with the authors, autographs from them and of course the auction itself—added another $3.1 million to the take, for a total of $4,765,100 for the onetime event.

June 21 brought the next major event—the statewide seventeen-theater Bond Premiere night. The participants and their premiere films (where available) were:

Ayers Theatre	*Higher and Higher*
Ball Theatre	unknown
Blue Hen Theatre	unknown
Capitol Theatre	*Pin-Up Girl*
Crest Theatre*	*What a Woman*
Diamond Theatre**	unknown
Earle Theatre	*Lady in the Dark*
Layton Theatre	*Rookies in Burma*
Lewes Auditorium	*Meet the People*
Milton Theatre	unknown
National Theatre	*The Fighting Seabees*
New Waller Theatre**	unknown
Schine's New Plaza**	*The Eve of St. Mark*
Pike Theatre*	*Hi Diddle Diddle*
State Theatre	*Lady in the Dark*
Strand Theatre (Smyrna)	unknown
Warner Theatre	*Up in Arms*

*Due to previous commitments, this premiere occurred on June 25.
**This premiere was unexpectedly postponed to a later date.

On June 21, 1944, Wilmington's Warner Theatre held a bond premiere as part of the Fifth War Loan Drive. Sixteen other theaters in the state held similar premieres of different movies that night or shortly after. *Delaware Public Archives.*

The centerpiece of the night, of course, was the Warner premiere. Before screening *Up in Arms* starring Danny Kaye and Dinah Shore, the theater entertained the capacity crowd with a live show of singers and musicians straight from Fort DuPont. By the time the night was over, the Warner had amassed $1.425 million in bond sales. Some of the other theaters fared as follows: Ayers $47,000; Capitol $87,500; Crest $4,425; Earle $15,750; Layton $50,425; Lewes Auditorium $5,200; Pike $4,590; and State Theatre $57,000.

But in the middle of all those premieres and all that money was a pretty great personal story out of Claymont.

Richard Edge was the manager of the Pike Theatre when he joined the military around late 1942. His mother and stepfather helped run the business in his absence, but he always stayed connected to the theater, either by mail or by visits when he had leave. He was a member of a coast artillery unit stationed at Fort Adams (Rhode Island) when he learned of the multi-theater premiere event for the Fifth War Loan Drive. Not only did he want the Pike Theatre to be involved, but he wanted to be involved as well. He made arrangements for a furlough so he could personally oversee the event. He also went a step further and screened *The Deerslayer*, starring Bruce Kellogg, during the day that Sunday, for any child who bought at least one dollar in war stamps, and then followed up that night with the premiere screening of *Hi Diddle Diddle*.

The Hollywood-fueled fundraising continued the next day (June 22) with a star-studded event that served not only as a bond rally but also as a dedication of the Court of Flags of the United Nations at Rodney Square. An estimated crowd of thirty thousand—one-quarter of the city's population and with a ratio reported to be fifty women for each man—attended.

The ceremony included the raising of the flags and an impassioned speech by U.S. Air Force war hero Major Allen V. Martini, but it was the celebrities that folks came to see and see them they did. Leading the group that traveled in a "jeeparade" (driven by men from Fort DuPont) from the train station to

This "jeeparade" of stars is on its way from the Wilmington Train Station to the dedication of the Court of Flags of the United Nations at Rodney Square as part of Fifth War Loan Drive events in June 1944. Actor Mischa Auer is in the second jeep, adjusting his sunglasses. *Delaware Public Archives.*

Ilene Woods and bandleader Paul Whiteman (here directing the Air Force Technical Command Band) perform for thirty thousand people after the dedication of the Court of Flags of the United Nations at Rodney Square, all part of the Fifth War Loan Drive (June 1944). *Delaware Public Archives.*

the Hotel DuPont to the rally was actor Mischa Auer (*My Man Godfrey*, *Destry Rides Again*), who served as the evening's master of ceremonies. Leading the Army Air Force Technical Command Band was musician/bandleader Paul Whiteman—dubbed the "King of Jazz" by Duke Ellington. Performing musical numbers with the band were singers Rosemary Lane (of the Lane Sisters) and future voice of Walt Disney's *Cinderella* Ilene Woods. Rounding out the celeb group were dancer Johnny Coy, B-movie leading man Dennis O'Keefe, actor John Payne (*Sun Valley Serenade* and later *Miracle on 34th Street*) and future Oscar winner (Best Actor, *Stalag 17*) William Holden; Holden and Payne were in the military at the time.

Among the three AWVS-staffed bond booths and the two hundred retail salesclerks canvassing the crowd, $1.5 million in bonds were sold at that rally.

The last major movie event in the official Fifth War Loan Drive timeline was a Free Movie Day like those offered previously. This incarnation was staged on July 6 and was both national and statewide, offering free admission

There was a large turnout for the dedication of the Court of Flags of the United Nations at Rodney Square that took place during the Fifth War Loan Drive (June 1944). *Delaware Public Archives.*

to a film for each bond purchased. The theaters and their Fifth War Loan Drive "Free Movie Day" films (where available) were:

Ace Theatre	*Cover Girl*
Arcadia	*The Hour Before the Dawn*
Ayers Theatre	*Chip Off the Old Block*
Capitol Theatre	*Gaslight*
Crest Theatre	*Hat Check Honey* and *Moonlight in Vermont*
Earle Theatre	*Between Two Worlds*
Edge Moor Theatre	*Charlie Chan in the Chinese Cat* and *Up in Mabel's Room*
Grand Theatre	*Yellow Rose of Texas*
Layton Theatre	*Shot in the Escape* and *Tampico*
Loew's Aldine	*White Cliffs of Dover*
National Theatre	*In Our Time*

New Waller Theatre	*Buffalo Bill* and *Rosie the Riveter*
Palace Theatre	*Lady and the Monster* and *Oh, Susanna!*
Park Theatre	*Buffalo Bill*
Pike Theater	*Tender Comrade*
Queen Theatre	*Snow White and the Seven Dwarfs*
Rialto Theatre	*The Eve of St. Mark*
Ritz Theatre	*Beneath Western Skies* and *Juggernaut*
The Roxy	*The Hour Before the Dawn*
The Savoy	*The North Star*
Schine's New Plaza	*Henpecked Rooster* and *Two Girls and a Sailor*
State Theatre	*Henry Aldrich Haunts a House* and *Tunisian Victory*
The Strand (Wilmington)	*The Uninvited*
Strand Theatre (Smyrna)	*Outlaws of Santa Fe* and *The Uninvited*
Warner Theatre	*Going My Way*

At the end of the Fifth War Loan Drive, Delaware was $8 million short of its quota—only this time there was no delayed reporting. The state had until the end of July to make up the deficit. Milford's New Plaza Theatre would contribute to that as it was finally able to screen its bond premiere, but it would certainly take more than that premiere and a smattering of others to help. Delaware theaters stepped up one more time with a July 26 statewide Free Movie Day. The theaters and their second Fifth War Loan Drive "Free Movie Day" films (where available) were:

Ace Theatre	*Girl in the Case* and *Juggernaut*
Arcadia	*Days of Glory*
Ayers Theatre	*Make Your Own Bed*
Capitol Theatre	*The Eve of St. Mark*
Crest Theatre	*Hi, Good Lookin'* and *Weird Woman*
Earle Theatre	*Lady in the Dark*
Edge Moor Theatre	*The Falcon Out West* and *Kitty Foyle*
Grand Theatre	*The Monster Maker*
Layton Theatre	*Address Unknown*
Loew's Aldine	*The Hairy Ape*
National Theatre	*Four Jills in a Jeep*
New Waller Theatre	*Billy the Kid* and *Love Crazy*
Palace Theatre	*Show Boat* and *Transatlantic Tunnel*
Park Theatre	*The Uninvited*

Nothing gets attention like Nazi symbolism, especially when it's being swept away thanks to contributions to the Fifth War Loan Drive (1944). *National Archives and Records Administration.*

Pike Theater	*The Cowboy and the Senorita* and *The Falcon and the Co-Ed*
Queen Theatre	*The Adventures of Mark Twain*
Rialto Theatre	*Home in Indiana*
Ritz Theatre	*Meet the People*
The Roxy	*Hi, Good Lookin'*
The Savoy	*Gangway for Tomorrow* and *Rookies in Burma*
Schine's New Plaza	*Make Your Own Bed* and *Three Russian Girls*
State Theatre	*The Hour Before the Dawn*
The Strand (Wilmington)	*Jane Eyre*
Strand Theatre (Smyrna)	*Follow the Boys*
Warner Theatre	*Show Business*

One side note: a film produced by the War Department titled *Army Air Forces Report* was made available during the Fifth War Loan Drive, but only to workers in war-supporting industries. It showed, documentary-style, how in two years the U.S. Air Force went from the seventh-largest in the world to the largest. The film, available in 16mm and 35mm, was never released commercially; only war workers or civic groups could obtain a copy for screening. Additional footage filmed in the South Pacific, North Africa, Europe, and the Far East was also available to those groups.

By the end of July, Delaware had done it again, landing beyond its goal with $55.3 million, over $1 million more than asked, while the national quota was crushed, hitting $20.6 billion against its goal of $16 billion.

The Sixth War Loan Drive

(November 20, 1944, through December 16, 1944)

With America's direct involvement in World War II approaching three years, Uncle Sam again turned to the nation for financial help. The country's goal this time was $14 billion; of that, Delaware was asked to supply $48 million. The slogan was "Buy an Extra Bond."

As in drives past, retailers met at Wilmington's Queen Theatre to discuss strategies and goals. This drive brought a new twist, though: the creation of the "The Third Army." The thinking was that the "The First Army" was at the combat front and "The Second Army" was at the production front, leaving "The Third Army" to man the retail front. There was even a

A "bondmobile" offers curbside bond sales across the street from the Playhouse in Wilmington during the Sixth War Loan Drive (circa December 1944). *Delaware Public Archives.*

rank system. Every retailer began as a private, and as each man and woman sold bonds, they would be promoted up the ranks. Anyone selling $5,000 or more in bonds would become a full general. Some two thousand retail employees—owners, salesclerks, office staff and so on—were asked to take an oath of allegiance as part of their membership in the Third Army:

> *I, ______, do solemnly swear or affirm that I will bear true faith and allegiance to the United States of America and to the Third Bond Army which I will serve honestly and faithfully, devoting my time and best efforts to the successful completion of the Sixth War Loan Drive and that I will obey the orders of those appointed over me and to the best of my ability, will perform each act and duty assigned to me, so help me God.*

The overall strategy of the Sixth War Loan Drive focused less on splashy events and more on door-to-door canvassing, with 1,500 Treasury volunteers

As part of the Sixth War Loan Drive, retail employees are sworn in as members of "The Third Army" at the Queen Theatre (November 1944). *Delaware Public Archives.*

ready to go. This strategy was clearly reflected in theaters' activity; while booths continued to be manned for everyday bond sales, drive-specific events were kept to a minimum this go-round.

The most publicized film event took place on December 6, when Loew's Aldine held a war bond premiere of *Lost in a Harem* starring Abbott and Costello. Only a bond could get you in, but all city theaters sold bonds to that premiere. Before the film, Private First Class Stanley Hummel from Dover Army Air Base, a concert pianist before the war, gave a piano concert. About 1,800 people purchased almost $425,000 in bonds for that screening.

The next day, which was both Pearl Harbor Day and Delaware Day, offered another Free Movie Day event, although it was not statewide; in total, about half the state's theaters (including all Wilmington theaters) took part. The theaters and their Sixth War Loan Drive "Free Movie Day" films (where available) were:

Ace Theatre	*Mr. Skeffington*
Arcadia	*Youth Runs Wild*
Capitol Theatre	*Rainbow Island*
Crest Theatre	*The Big Noise* and *Cobra Woman*

Earle Theatre	*Barbary Coast Gent*
Edge Moor Theatre	*Since You Went Away*
Grand Theatre	*Rustler's Hideout*
Loew's Aldine	*3 Is a Family*
National Theatre	*Arsenic and Old Lace*
New Waller Theatre	*Her Primitive Man* and *In the Meantime, Darling*
Park Theatre	*Mask of Dimitrios* and *Taxi, Mister*
Queen Theatre	*The Master Race*
Rialto Theatre	*Laura*
Ritz Theatre	*Marked Trails* and *Seven Sweethearts*
The Savoy	*Ladies Courageous*
Schine's New Plaza	*Pardon My Rhythm*
The Strand (Wilmington)	*Song of the Open Road*
Strand Theatre (Smyrna)	*Goin' to Town* and *Laramie Trail*
Warner Theatre	*Our Hearts Were Young and Gay*

During the Sixth War Loan Drive, this bond booth offered Disney-branded war bond "gift certificates" for bonds purchased as gifts for children (circa December 1944). *Delaware Public Archives.*

UNITED STATES TREASURY

WAR FINANCE COMMITTEE

Know All Men By These Presents:

This is to certify that ______________________
is the owner of a War Bond, thereby becoming an investor in this country's fight for human liberty and a contributor in a world struggle to make life free and forever peaceful for all men.

This Bond presented by: ______________________

Attested this ________ day of ________ 194__

This is a replica of the Disney-branded war bond "gift certificate" offered during the December 1944 Sixth War Loan Drive. *From the author's personal collection.*

A few other individual bond premieres took place later during the Drive. Wilmington's Ritz and Park theaters screened *My Pal Wolf*, which were promoted as screenings for children, while for grown-ups in other towns there were bond premieres of *An American Romance* (New Plaza Theatre), *His Butler's Sister* (Earle Theatre), *Claudia* (Pike Theatre) and *Mr. Parkington* (Capitol Theatre). That Capitol event, though, was more than just a screening. There was an auction of enemy souvenirs, along with a live music performance by the Thunderbolts of the Dover Army Air Base (who played the Milford bond premiere the night before).

Once again, 16mm films made their way to people outside of theatrical channels thanks to the establishment of what news items dubbed a "16mm movie circuit." If any club or organization in the state wanted to have the Sixth War Loan Drive explained to their members, that group could contact a speakers' bureau established by the Delaware War Finance Committee. Also available were short 16mm "semi-restricted" War Department sound films depicting actual combat and other stark scenes. Available titles included:

This poster, which isn't subtle, would have coincided with the Sixth War Loan Drive (1944). *National Archives and Records Administration.*

The 957th Day, showing combat action in the Pacific
Just for Remembrance, showing dead Americans on a Pacific battlefield
The Line Is Busy, which stresses the importance of not missing work
Photography Flights, which spotlights the navy's photographic interpretation team
Silence, showing battlefield wreckage
Two and a Half Minutes, showing men falling in battle or being attended to by corpsmen

The Sixth War Loan Drive was a massive success, collecting $21.6 billion nationally and $58.4 million from Delaware efforts.

THE SEVENTH WAR LOAN DRIVE

(May 14, 1945, through June 30, 1945)

The "Mighty 7th," as it was called, was mighty indeed, at least in terms of duration. While the financial goals of the country ($14 billion) and the state ($43 million) were not the most ambitious of all the drives, the Seventh would be the longest drive to date: almost seven full weeks officially, with some efforts kicking off in April.

On the eve of that April pre-kickoff, Delaware's War Finance Committee convened at Wilmington's Hotel DuPont to discuss strategy. The first "wave," beginning on April 1, would focus first on automatic payroll deductions for employees at war plants and other places of employment (a practice that had been broadly successful for some time), followed by a concentration on public schools and then on door-to-door canvassing. One of the things attendees were treated to was an advance screening of the new documentary short *Fury in the Pacific*, which was produced by the army, navy and marine corps and depicted their joint attack on an island held by the Japanese.

Ongoing planning for the Seventh War Loan Drive's formal timeline included Hollywood star Binnie Barnes being tapped to direct war bond plays in Wilmington (see "The Stars: Celebrity Cameos in the First State," for more on how Barnes was involved there); a "War Bond Cruise" aboard the USS *American Seaman*, where anyone who bought at least a $1,000 bond could take a five-hour tour along the Delaware River in the U.S. Maritime Service vessel; and a series of war shows around the state, from Claymont to Rehoboth.

A 10 percent payroll deduction is nothing to take lightly, but seeing Hitler and Göring as cartoon buffoons helps reduce the sting of the immediate financial sacrifice (undated). *National Archives and Records Administration.*

Less than a week before the formal kickoff of the Mighty 7th, Germany surrendered, and May 8 was deemed V-E Day (Victory in Europe Day). Despite this success, and despite the first wave of the campaign having already collected $8 million in bond sales (which would hit $9 million by May 14), organizers were quick to address that the job wasn't over—that Japan was the country that bombed Pearl Harbor and it was still a threat. The public would respond.

Once again, Wilmington's Queen Theatre was the site of the kickoff meeting, this time attended by some 1,200 retailers who pledged to "Pour out our might for the Mighty 7th." In addition to a speech by Wilmington mayor Albert James, the attendees heard talks from Major Mike Frankovich, executive officer of New Castle Army Air Base, and his wife, actress Binnie

Actress Ida Lupino promotes Free Movie Day during the Seventh War Loan Drive (June 1945). *Delaware Public Archives.*

Barnes. Folks also heard tunes from the Skymeisters of the New Castle Army Air Base. That evening, forty thousand people lined the city streets to watch a military parade.

Buried beneath the (well-deserved) opening-day hype of the meeting at the Queen and the parade in the city was the opening of the Seventh War Loan Theatre, located in the auditorium of the Wilmington Public Library. Every afternoon from 12:30 to 2:00, the Delaware War Finance Committee would host public screenings of war pictures—actual footage from the war, with a focus on the Pacific—for free.

The major theaters, beyond the Loew's Aldine giving away a color photo of marines raising the American flag at Iwo Jima (yes, *that* picture) to the first one hundred people who bought a bond on May 16, did very little outside the norm until June 6, when every theater in the state hosted another Free Movie Day. The theaters and their Seventh War Loan Drive "Free Movie Day" films (where available) were:

Ace Theatre	*Exile Express* and *Irene*
Arcadia	*Salty O'Rourke*
Ayers Theatre	*Song of Bernadette*
Capitol Theatre	*Murder My Sweet*
Crest Theatre	*Address Unknown* and *Night Club Girl*
Earle Theatre	*Since You Went Away*
Edge Moor Theatre	*A Song to Remember*
Grand Theatre	*The Crime Doctor's Courage* and *The Navajo Trail*
Layton Theatre	*Dog Watch* and *Tiger Trouble* and *God Is My Co-Pilot*
Loew's Aldine	*Without Love*
National Theatre	*The Keys of the Kingdom*
New Waller Theatre	*Her Lucky Night* and *Royal Scandal*

Palace Theatre	*Dark Waters* and *A Guy, a Gal, and a Pal*
Park Theatre	*Going My Way*
Pike Theater	*A Girl, a Guy, and a Gob*
Queen Theatre	*Youth Aflame*
Rialto Theatre	*Where Do We Go from Here*
Ritz Theatre	*Experiment Perilous*
The Roxy	*High Powered*
The Savoy	*Moonlight and Cactus* and *Rogues' Gallery*
Schine's New Plaza	*Bachelor Mother* and *No News Is Good News* and *Suspicion*
State Theatre	*To Have and Have Not*
The Strand (Wilmington)	*A Tree Grows in Brooklyn*
Strand Theatre (Smyrna)	*The West Coast Question* (A *March of Time* Newsreel) and *Can't Help Singing*
Warner Theatre	*The Affairs of Susan*

This Seventh War Loan Drive poster looks similar to the famous picture of men raising the flag at Iwo Jima, surely by design (1945). *National Archives and Records Administration.*

Several weeks later, the Warner held a bond premiere of the film-noir *Conflict*, starring Humphrey Bogart and Sidney Greenstreet, while another premiere at the Capitol was *Without Love*, a romantic comedy starring Spencer Tracy and Katharine Hepburn.

When the Mighty 7th came to a close, the final numbers were, well, pretty mighty. The country's goal of $14 billion was nearly doubled at $26 billion. The state goal of $43 million could make a similar claim, delivering $75.8 million.

Across all seven drives, Delaware companies, organizations, citizens and theaters raised $391.2 million. In 2022 dollars, that's about $6.4 billion.

In less than three years.

THE MANAGERS

Homefront Field Commanders Leading the Stateside Charge

Delaware movie theater managers did more than show movies. They were businessmen and church leaders and caretakers and politicians. They said hello to babies and goodbye to elders. They had full-time jobs, families and loved ones overseas. They rationed gas and collected scrap and donated clothing. They invested in bonds and stamps, and they donated to charities. They worried at night for the safety of their children. Some even went off to battle. In these aspects, theater managers were just like everyone else in World War II Delaware.

But that's where the comparisons stop. Unlike other folks of this era, this Band of Exhibitor Brothers gave tirelessly to their communities by way of forming or joining clubs, serving on committees, liaising with Hollywood, liaising with the military and meeting with community leaders and community members alike. These managers invested countless hours to ensure every child received a toy, every patron bought a bond and every polio victim had a chance. They also made the local gossip column on a regular basis for what they were doing in town, what they were screening at work and where they were going on vacation.

Yes, they were competitors screening movies, but they were also partners helping the war effort.

The information that follows is a representative list of the organizations and committees Delaware theater managers formed or joined to improve something for someone else—everything from improving a screening to

Donald Ross (*center left*), War Savings Staff state administrator, presents Lewis Black, Warner Theatre manager, with a Minute Men Award for cooperation in the sale of war bonds. Surrounding them are the city's other theater managers who were also recipients of the award (January 1943). *Delaware Public Archives*.

improving a life. Where no title is listed, general membership is implied, and where managers served the same organization over multiple years, or where they held multiple positions within the same organization over time, I selected only one entry in the interest of space.

It's an impressive list.

Harry Aumack, The Roxy

Smyrna Business Association Food Matinee Citizens Committee
Smyrna Holiday Parade Committee

Thomas Ayers, Sussex Theatre/Ayers Theatre, Layton Theatre

Georgetown War Bond Sales Community Committee
March of Dimes Executive Committee (Sussex County Motion Pictures Co-Chairman)

Salute to Our Heroes Bond and Stamp Drive (Kent County Motion Pictures Co-Chairman)
Seaford *Rollin' Abroad* Program Subcommittee
Seaford WAC Recruiting Committee

A.J. Belair, Rialto Theatre
Fifth War Loan Drive (New Castle County Motion Pictures Chairman)
Delaware War Activities Committee (New Castle County Motion Pictures Chairman)
March of Dimes (Delaware Motion Pictures Chairman)
Miss Victory Committee of Theater Managers
Wilmington Community Christmas Committee
Wilmington and New Castle County Free Movie Day Committee
Young Men's Republican Club Board of Governors
Recipient, Minute Men Award (for cooperation in the sale of war bonds)

Walter "Huck" Betts, Ball Theatre
David Grayson Club of the Future Farmers of America (Laurel Chapter Vice President)
Frankford War Price and Rationing Board (Chairman)
March of Dimes (Delaware Motion Pictures Advisory Committee)
Millsboro Lions Club (President)
Millsboro Red Cross Branch (Chairman)
Millsboro Tire Rationing Board
Sussex County Layman's League (President)

Birk Binnard, Queen Theatre
March of Dimes Press and Publications Committee (Delaware Motion Pictures)

Lewis Black, Warner Theatre
Sixth War Loan Drive (State Coordinator)
Seventh War Loan Million Dollar Bond Cruise Committee
Army and Navy Relief Fund (New Castle County Motion Pictures Chairman)
Defense Savings Committee (Delaware Motion Pictures Representative)
Delaware Safety Council Board of Directors

Delaware State Committee of the American Cancer Society
Delaware War Activities Committee (Motion Pictures Division Chairman)
Delaware War Bond Committee (Motion Pictures Chairman)
Greek War Relief Fund Benefit Screening Publicity Committee
March of Dimes (Delaware Motion Pictures Vice-Chairman)
Miss Victory Committee of Theater Managers
Salute to Our Heroes Bond and Stamp Drive (Delaware Motion Pictures Chairman)
Theatre Managers Club of Wilmington (President)
WAC Anniversary Week (Wilmington Co-Chairman)
Wilmington Advertising Club
Wilmington Air Raid Wardens (Chief Deputy, Recreations and Amusements)
Wilmington Book and Authors Rally Publicity Relations Committee
Wilmington Campaign for Conservation of Critical Resources (Mayor's Committee)
Wilmington Chamber of Commerce
Wilmington Community Christmas Committee
Wilmington Dedication of the Court of Flags of the United Nations Welcoming Committee
Wilmington Theatre Managers Association (President)
Wilmington WAC Recruiting Committee
Recipient, Minute Men Award (for cooperation in the sale of war bonds)

ANTHONY JOSEPH (A.J.) DEFIORE, PARK THEATRE
Fourth War Loan Drive (New Castle County Motion Pictures Chairman)
Fifth War Loan Drive (Delaware Motion Pictures Co-Chairman)
Sixth War Loan Drive (Delaware Motion Pictures Chairman)
Seventh War Loan (Delaware Motion Pictures Chairman)
Army and Navy Relief Fund (Delaware Motion Pictures Chairman)
Avenge Pearl Harbor on Delaware Day (New Castle County Motion Pictures Chairman)
Christopher Columbus Society War Bond Campaign (Wilmington Campaign and Publicity Chairman)
Delaware Motion Picture Committee for National Defense
Delaware Motion Picture Committee / War Savings Staff (Liaison for Paulette Goddard's Appearance)
Delaware State Council for Defense (Press and Public Relations Committee)
Governor's Committee on Post-War Problems (Small Business)

Independent Motion Picture Theatre Operators of Delaware and the Eastern Shore of Maryland (Founder)
March of Dimes (Delaware Motion Pictures Chairman)
Miss Victory Committee of Theater Managers
Red Cross Motion Picture Committee for Delaware Theatre War Activities (Chairman)
Red Cross War Fund Drive (Delaware Motion Pictures Chairman)
Salute to Our Heroes Bond and Stamp Drive (New Castle County Motion Pictures Chairman)
Theatre Managers Club of Wilmington (Secretary-Treasurer)
United War Fund Drive (Delaware Motion Pictures Co-Chairman)
Wilmington Air Raid Wardens (Assistant Chief Deputy, Recreations and Amusements)
Wilmington Community Christmas Committee
Wilmington and New Castle County Free Movie Day Committee
Wilmington Salvage Drive (Sub-Chairman)
Wilmington Sixth District Assistant Warden
WAC Anniversary Week (Wilmington Co-Chairman)
WAC Recruiting Committee (Wilmington Chairman)
Recipient, Minute Men Award (for cooperation in the sale of war bonds)

A.J. DeFiore, Park Theatre manager and Delaware Motion Pictures chairman for the March of Dimes campaign (*center*), poses with radio performers Monica Lewis and Danny O'Neill at the January 1945 Parade of Stars event at Wilmington's Armory. *Delaware Public Archives.*

William B. Derrickson, Avenue Theatre

March of Dimes Advisory Committee (Delaware Motion Pictures)
Rehoboth Citizen's Sixth War Loan Drive Committee

Edgar J. Doob, Loew's Theatre, Loew's Aldine Theatre

Sixth War Loan Drive (Delaware Motion Pictures Publicity Chairman)
Seventh War Loan Million Dollar Bond Cruise Committee
American Legion Laurence Roberts Post, No. 21
Army and Navy Relief Fund (New Castle County Motion Pictures Coordinator)
Delaware Motion Picture Group (Publicity Chairman)
Delaware War Activities Committee (Motion Pictures Publicity Chairman, State Coordinator)
Greek War Relief Fund Benefit Screening Publicity Committee
March of Dimes (Delaware Motion Pictures Coordinator, Vice Chairman and Director of Public Relations)
Miss Victory Committee of Theater Managers
New Castle County War Bond Committee (Motion Pictures Co-Chairman)
Red Cross Motion Picture Committee for Delaware Theatre War Activities (Vice-Chairman)
Red Cross Theater Participation (Delaware Coordinator)
Salute to Our Heroes Bond and Stamp Drive (Delaware Motion Pictures Publicity Chairman)
Toys for Every Needy Child Campaign (Wilmington's Hospital Committee Head)
United War Fund Drive (Delaware Motion Pictures Co-Chairman)
Victory Bond Campaign (Delaware Motion Pictures Publicity Chairman)
War Bond Premiere Committee, *A Yank at Eton* (Chairman)
Wilmington Air Raid Wardens (Assistant, Recreations and Amusements)
Wilmington Community Christmas Committee
Wilmington Dedication of the Court of Flags of the United Nations Welcoming Committee
Wilmington and New Castle County Free Movie Day Committee
Wilmington Theatre Managers Club (Vice President)
Wilmington WAC Recruiting Committee
Recipient, Honored Hundred Award (top one hundred in E-Bond sales in the country during the Fourth War Loan Drive)
Recipient, Minute Men Award (for cooperation in the sale of war bonds)

Edward Evans, Schine's New Plaza Theatre

Fourth War Loan Drive (Sussex County Motion Pictures Chairman)

Sixth War Loan Drive (Delaware Motion Pictures Vice-Chairman)

Army Emergency Relief Fund Ticket Committee for Milford's *This Is the Army* benefit screening

Democratic State Convention Delegate

Delaware Motion Picture Committee for National Defense

Delaware War Activities Committee (Kent and Sussex Counties Motion Pictures Chairman)

Independent Motion Picture Theatre Operators of Delaware and the Eastern Shore of Maryland

March of Dimes (Kent County Motion Picture Co-Chairman, Sussex County Motion Picture Chairman)

Milford Aluminum Drive (Head)

Milford Bond Drive Committee

Milford Chamber of Commerce (Director)

Milford Civilian Defense (Director)

Milford Halloween Community Festival (Chairman)

Milford Mayor

Milford WAC Recruiting Committee (Chairman)

Red Cross Theater Collection, April 1944 (Kent and Sussex Counties Chairman)

Sussex County Chief Blackout Coordinator

Sussex County Civilian Defense Coordinator

Sussex County Free Movie Day Committee (Chairman)

Sussex County Rubber Drive Coordinator

Sussex County Scrap Salvage Chairman

Sussex County War Bond Chairman

Earle Finney, The Savoy

Greek War Relief Fund Benefit Screening Display Committee

March of Dimes Advisory Committee (Delaware Motion Pictures)

Miss Victory Committee of Theater Managers

Wilmington Air Raid Wardens (Assistant, Recreations and Amusements)

Wilmington Community Christmas Committee

Wilmington Toy for Every Child Drive Committee (Motion Pictures Chairman)

Recipient, Minute Men Award (for cooperation in the sale of war bonds)

Albert J. Fischer, Edge Moor Theatre
Delaware Motion Picture Committee for National Defense
Independent Motion Picture Theatre Operators of Delaware and the Eastern Shore of Maryland
Miss Victory Committee of Theater Managers

Louis Handloff, State Theatre
Delaware Motion Picture Committee for National Defense
Independent Motion Picture Theatre Operators of Delaware and the Eastern Shore of Maryland
Jewish Federation of Delaware (Director)
Newark United National Clothing Collection Campaign Special Events Committee
Red Cross War Fund Campaign Member
United Jewish Campaign (Downstate Leader)
Young Men's and Young Women's Hebrew Association (Lower Delaware Representative)

Reese Harrington, Reese Theatre
Delaware Theatre Bond Drive, May 1942 (Kent County Co-Chairman)
March of Dimes Executive Committee (Delaware Motion Pictures)
Salute to Our Heroes Bond and Stamp Drive (Kent County Motion Pictures Co-Chairman)

Raymond Harris, Playhouse
Wilmington Air Raid Wardens (Assistant, Recreations and Amusements)

John O Hopkins, National Theatre
Third War Loan Arrangements Committee
Delaware Motion Picture Committee for National Defense
Delaware State Conference on Employment Problems for the Negro, Conference Planning Committee
Governor Bacon's Statewide Committee on Post-War Problems
Independent Motion Picture Theatre Operators of Delaware and the Eastern Shore of Maryland

March of Dimes Executive Committee (Delaware Motion Pictures)
NAACP Membership Drive Team Captain
Walnut Street Christian Association Gifts Committee for the "Walnut Street 'Y' Campaign"
Wilmington City Councilman
Wilmington Community Christmas Committee

Charles Horn, Blue Hen Theatre, Lewes Auditorium
Sixth War Loan Lewes Theater Committee
All Saints Church Vestryman
American Legion Boy Scout Committee
Coast Guard Auxiliary Unit Flotilla No. 42
Henlopen Post No. 5
Lewes Chamber of Commerce (Director)
Lewes and Rehoboth Beach Motion Pictures Exhibitors Campaign (Chairman)
March of Dimes Executive Committee (Sussex County Motion Pictures Co-Chairman)
Rehoboth Beach Chamber of Commerce (Publicity Committee)
Rehoboth Beach Kiwanis Club Director
Rehoboth Citizen's Committee (Sixth War Loan)
Rehoboth High School Alumni Association (Corresponding Secretary)
Sussex County Layman's League (Vice President)

Richard Kirsh, Queen Theatre
March of Dimes Publicity and Special Events Committee (Delaware Motion Pictures)
Miss Victory Committee of Theater Managers
Salute to Our Heroes Bond and Stamp Drive (New Castle County Motion Pictures Publicity Chairman)
War Bond Premiere Committee, *A Yank at Eton*
Wilmington Air Raid Wardens (Assistant, Recreations and Amusements)
Wilmington Community Christmas Committee
Recipient, Minute Men Award (for cooperation in the sale of war bonds)

A.J. DeFiore (*left foreground*), Park Theatre manager and Delaware Motion Pictures chairman for the March of Dimes campaign, presents Jesse S. Cooper, state chairman of the Infantile Paralysis Committee, with a check for $2,773.18 from the Wilmington motion picture theaters in 1943. In the picture behind the principals and representing the city's theaters are James Olwell (Rialto), Frederic R. Gibbs (Ace), Lee Levy (Arcadia), Birk Binnard (Queen), Lewis Black (Warner), Edgar J. Doob (Loew's) and Earle G. Finney (Savoy). *Delaware Public Archives.*

JOHN KOZAK, EARLE THEATRE

March of Dimes Advisory Committee (Delaware Motion Pictures)

FRED LEOPOLD, GRAND THEATRE

Wilmington Community Christmas Committee

LEE LEVY, ARCADIA THEATRE

Greek War Relief Fund Benefit Screening Display Committee
March of Dimes Publicity and Special Events Committee (Delaware Motion Pictures)
Miss Victory Committee of Theater Managers
Wilmington Air Raid Wardens (Assistant, Recreations and Amusements)
Wilmington Community Christmas Committee "Toy for Every Child" Drive
Recipient, Minute Men Award (for cooperation in the sale of war bonds)

SIDNEY MUNTER, GRAND THEATRE, RITZ THEATRE, QUEEN THEATRE, ARCADIA THEATRE

Greek War Relief Fund Benefit Screening Ticket Committee
Miss Victory Committee of Theater Managers
Wilmington Air Raid Wardens (Assistant, Recreations and Amusements)
Recipient, Minute Men Award (for cooperation in the sale of war bonds)

ELMER PICKARD, RITZ THEATRE
Wilmington Air Raid Wardens (Assistant, Recreations and Amusements)

GEORGE SCHWARTZ, CAPITOL THEATRE, EVERETT THEATRE, STRAND THEATRE, TEMPLE THEATRE
Delaware Theatre Bond Drive, May 1942 (Kent County Co-Chairman)

MURIEL SCHWARTZ, CAPITOL THEATRE, EVERETT THEATRE, STRAND THEATRE, TEMPLE THEATRE
March of Dimes Advisory Committee (Delaware Motion Pictures)

REBA SCHWARTZ, CAPITOL THEATRE, EVERETT THEATRE, STRAND THEATRE, TEMPLE THEATRE
March of Dimes Advisory Committee (Delaware Motion Pictures)

BENJAMIN SELIGMAN, STRAND, WILMINGTON
Delaware Motion Picture Committee for National Defense
Greek War Relief Fund Benefit Screening Publicity Committee
Independent Motion Picture Theatre Operators of Delaware and the Eastern Shore of Maryland
March of Dimes Executive Committee (Delaware Motion Pictures)
Miss Victory Committee of Theater Managers
War Bond Premiere Committee, *A Yank at Eton*
Wilmington Air Raid Wardens (Assistant, Recreations and Amusements)
Recipient, Minute Men Award (for cooperation in the sale of war bonds)

SYLVAN SHAVITZ, CREST THEATRE
March of Dimes Advisory Committee (Delaware Motion Pictures)

BENJAMIN SHINDLER, ACE THEATRE, CREST THEATRE
Brandywine Country Club Board of Governors
Delaware Motion Picture Committee for National Defense

Independent Motion Picture Theatre Operators of Delaware and the Eastern Shore of Maryland
Independent Order of B'nai B'rith (Wilmington Lodge) Americanization Committee
Jewish Welfare Organization National Council of the Joint Distribution Committee
March of Dimes (Delaware Motion Pictures Chairman)
Miss Victory Committee of Theater Managers
Salute to Our Heroes Bond and Stamp Drive (New Castle County Motion Pictures Advance War Bond Sale Chairman)
Temple Beth Shalom (Director)
Theatre Managers Club of Wilmington (Vice President)
United Jewish Campaign Businessmen's Division
Wilmington Air Raid Wardens (Assistant, Recreations and Amusements)
Wilmington Community Christmas Committee "Toy for Every Child" Drive
Wilmington and New Castle County Free Movie Day Committee (Publicity Chairman)
Recipient, Minute Men Award (for cooperation in the sale of war bonds)

Three Wilmington theater managers discuss the July 26 "Free Movie Day" plans during 1944's Fifth War Loan Drive (*left to right*): A.J. DeFiore (Park Theatre), Lewis Black (Warner Theatre) and A.J. Belair (Rialto). *Delaware Public Archives.*

Ervin Snellenberg, Capitol Theatre
Fourth War Loan Drive (Kent County Motion Pictures Chairman)
Free Movie Day, July 1944 (Kent County Motion Pictures Chairman)
March of Dimes (Kent County Motion Pictures Chairman)
Motion Picture War Activities Committee (Kent County Chairman)
WAC Anniversary Week (Kent County Motion Pictures Chairman)

Helen Tindall, Ritz Theatre
March of Dimes Advisory Committee (Delaware Motion Pictures)

Roland Waller, Waller Theatre
Laurel Rotary Club

THE CARE PACKAGES

Providing Comfort in a Time of Crisis

As illustrated in "The Short Before the Feature: Theaters Help Between Poland and Pearl Harbor," prewar fundraising efforts were focused on more personal and humanitarian aid, as Delawareans and Delaware theaters helped everyone from nations around the world to neighbors around the block. After December 7, 1941, more focus shifted toward helping America fund the war via bond and stamp drives. While there was plenty of that (see "The War Loan Drives: Financing the Fight Through Film"), there were still efforts made to keep global and local relief initiatives going strong, whether continuing them from prewar efforts or starting something new.

Foreign Aid

Unlike prewar efforts, when theaters were involved in raising money for multiple individual countries like Poland, Finland, England, Greece and so on, wartime assistance to foreign countries was about pooling resources; thus was founded the United War Fund of Delaware, established to collect and distribute funds to groups in one of three areas: homefront (from the Boys' Club to the YWCA), military front (including the USO), and United Nations Relief Front (all those prewar countries and more). It ran from late 1943 at least through 1945, and theaters got in on the effort.

A frequent participant in United War Fund–related events was Wilmington's Playhouse. The storied theater hosted fundraisers, including a political lecture by NBC commentator Richard Harkness, a performance by Norwegian singer Nancy Ness and a concert by the Wilmington Symphony Orchestra; plus it was the site of the 1945 kickoff meeting for the organization. Other theaters involved in UWF efforts included the Crest, which allowed the Richardson Park School to raise funds there, and the Earle, which allowed William Penn High School to do the same.

One interesting screening note: when Claymont's United War Fund volunteers needed to meet for their instructions, they did not use the Pike Theatre; instead, they met in the Claymont Firehouse where they watched a couple of short pictures related to the war effort: *Here Come the Yanks* and *We Have a Job To Do*.

The Wilmington Drama League got in on the act as well, raising money for the UWF with a benefit performance of *My Sister Eileen* in October 1944. (They would take the same show on the road with a non-UWF, one-night-only performance at the Dover Army Air Field Theatre in November.)

Because of the centralized nature of the UWF's efforts, as well as the need for so many other resources, country-specific fundraising was not common, but there is evidence that before the start of the UWF in October 1943, and sometime around the end of its initial campaign in December 1944, a few Russian War Relief benefit items appeared, mostly at the Ace Theatre. The benefit screenings included the films *Russian Folk Dances*, *Yellow Caesar* (about Mussolini) and *This Is the Enemy* (a dramatization of Europe's resistance to Hitler). The Edge Moor Theatre did its part by collecting clothing donations.

Speaking of clothing, the City of Newark collected it to be sent to war-torn areas of the world; the State Theatre was both a drop-off point for any clothing donation, as well as host of a 1945 children's matinee where the price of a ticket was five pounds of clothes. That event contributed to the town's ten-ton collection of clothing. Other theaters participated in various clothing collections as well, including the Palace, New Waller and Capitol (which screened *A Guy Named Joe* as part of the collection effort).

ORGANIZATIONAL SUPPORT

With so many other fundraising efforts going on, it's hard to imagine theaters had time for one more, but they did, and with the exception of bond sales, it was their biggest ongoing effort during the war: the March of Dimes.

About a dozen years before he became president, Franklin Roosevelt contracted polio. Several years later, he founded a nonprofit that would become the National Foundation for Infantile Paralysis in 1937. Celebrity Eddie Cantor, along with others at Warner Bros. and MGM, had been tapped by Roosevelt to develop a fundraising strategy. During a meeting at MGM, Cantor coined the phrase "March of Dimes" as a play on words of the popular newsreel series *The March of Time*. That moniker still stands today, more than eighty years later.

In 1942, the motion picture industry promised to play a greater role in supporting the March of Dimes, and theaters were a big part of that. In connection with FDR's sixtieth birthday, the 1942 March of Dimes campaign ran from January 22 to 29, and the Delaware executive and publicity/special events committees were a who's who of Delaware theater managers. The money raised by each theater would be split 50/50: half would go to the national campaign and the other half would stay in each theater's community.

The campaign, which kicked off with a short promotional film starring Clark Gable, was a success. In addition to the placement of wishing well–shaped collection receptacles in theater lobbies and ushers soliciting donations throughout the day and night, special events—like the New Waller working with Laurel High School to assign kids to collect money from passersby in the street, and the four-hundred-person theater party at the Reese in Harrington—added to the statewide total of $5,782.90 in donations collected by theaters alone, more than one-third of the $13,066.13 collected around the state. The following year would be even better, with theaters collecting $6,736.30 as part of Delaware's overall showing of $14,804.45.

Specific March of Dimes screenings that took place in those early years were *The Man Who Came to Dinner* (starring Bette Davis) at the Reese in 1942 and *Forever and a Day* (with Victor McLaglen and Arthur Treacher) at the Crest in 1943.

"Make It More in '44" was the slogan the year after that, and make it more theaters did. With the help of the New Castle County Women's Committee manning theater collection booths, the state's military bases chipping in, events like a dance in the National Theatre building and a filmed plea from star Greer Garson, both theaters and the state surpassed their highs again, with thirty-one movie houses raising $17,360.29 as more than half of Delaware's total take of $30,151.39. That effort put Delaware as the top state in the country (and only second behind Washington, D.C.)

in terms of money raised per capita. It also earned Park Theatre manager and March of Dimes state chair A.J. DeFiore a trip to the White House to meet FDR. But the state and its theaters weren't done yet.

In 1945, firing on all cylinders and getting a fundraising boost from the Parade of Stars at the New Castle Army Air Base (see "The Stars: Celebrity Cameos in the First State"), theaters in Delaware shattered all previous records by collecting $23,298.55 as part of the state's overall haul of $45,017.52. And once again, DeFiore went to Washington, this time to meet President Truman and to discuss the 1946 campaign.

The March of Dimes wasn't the only familiar cause theaters supported; they also supported the Red Cross and the Red Cross War Fund. The biggest way they did this was with collection events. These were not screening-based events like bond premieres but rather specific weeklong efforts to make people aware of the Red Cross by way of lobby promotions, greeters and speakers; donations were collected in the process. In April 1943, Smyrna's Roxy and Strand theaters participated along with all Wilmington theaters; in 1944, a similar week was held, and most theaters in the state joined in. In 1945, all theaters in the state participated.

There were some one-off events, however. In mid-1944, the Capitol offered a live show for the benefit of the Red Cross Camp and Hospital Council. That show, produced by Bellanca Aircraft Corporation employees, was a minstrel show and amateur radio hour titled *Darktown Follies*. Earlier in 1944, the Loew's Aldine was at it with a screening of the propaganda film *Brothers in Blood* as part of a Red Cross donor drive. And in March 1945, the Earle held a Red Cross benefit matinee for kids.

There was smaller, targeted theatrical support, too. In 1943, on the stage of the Loew's Aldine, Governor Bacon inducted five Red Cross nurses into the army. Later that year, the Red Cross's "three-fold nursing program" (recruit nurses for service in the armed forces / enlist volunteers for nurse's aide training / enroll men and women in home nursing classes) was also promoted at the Arcadia, Loew's Aldine, Warner, Rialto, Savoy and Queen theaters. In August 1944, Milford's New Plaza hosted speakers between screenings to promote an army-navy blood bank drive, and in March 1945, Admiral William F. Halsey Jr., commander of the South Pacific forces and the Third Fleet, made a personal appearance at a Red Cross rally at the Playhouse.

Military Support

For our boys in mid-1942, the Navy Relief Society raised over $25,000 via many events that culminated with a roller-skating party at the rink on the estate of R.R.M. Carpenter. Theaters got in on the act. Across the state, the short film *A Sailor Speaks* was screened for theatergoers, who were then asked to contribute to the Relief Society. Students at the Seaford School sold tickets to a benefit screening at the Layton, and girls in sailor hats sold buttons in front of the Capitol.

Expanding those efforts shortly after that campaign, Delaware's theaters joined fifteen thousand other theaters around the country to raise money for the Army and Navy Emergency Relief Fund, where the plan was for ushers to collect donations from theater patrons while short films were shown.

In February 1943, it was reported that Irving Berlin's live stage musical *This Is the Army* pulled in almost $2 million after a run in New York that began on July 4, 1942, and was followed by a small tour (that did not make it to Delaware). All proceeds went to Army Emergency Relief, a fund set up to provide unexpected financial assistance to soldiers and their families whenever needed, with the thinking being that a soldier without financial worries is a better soldier.

When Hollywood took that play and turned it into a major motion picture with the same title, the Warner played host to the state's August 18 premiere, and what a premiere it was.

Ticket prices ranged from $2.20 to $11.00 (that high number is about $186 today), and all seats were for sale; everyone agreed that no invited guests would receive any seats for free. The first ticket was purchased by Mrs. James Smith Ford of Wilmington. Ford was a Red Cross nurse in World War I, and her daughter, Ensign Ellen Ford, was one of Delaware's first women to join the WAVES.

The night began outside the theater with spotlights, a roped-off entrance, autograph-seekers and WDEL manager J. Gorman Walsh manning a microphone and introducing prominent political, military and social figures as they arrived. All 1,700-plus tickets had been sold (along with some extra standing-room-only tickets at $1.65 each), including a block of 50 tickets anonymously purchased by one person and donated to the New Castle Army Air Base. A trio of WACs welcomed people as they entered. Some 150 onlookers watched it all.

Members of the American Women's Voluntary Services sell tickets to the Delaware premiere of *This Is the Army* at the Warner Theatre (August 1943). *Delaware Public Archives.*

In the lobby, war bonds and war stamp corsages were sold, and then an all-soldier prologue took place before the screening—a prologue that included big names in base entertainment: Corporals David Fitzgibbon and Stanley Ross of Fort Miles, along with the Jive Bombers of the New Castle Army Air Base. (See "The Entertainment: Putting on a Show Over Here Before Shipping Off Over There" for more on Fitzgibbon, Ross and the Jive Bombers). Twelve men from Fort DuPont presented colors.

This Is the Army would play in October that year at other theaters in the state, including the Capitol, New Waller and New Plaza, all for the benefit of Army Emergency Relief. Each screening would offer its own live components as well (music, speakers and so on). In January 1944, the film made it to the Crest Theatre.

It was reported in March 1945 that national screenings of *This Is the Army* raised a combined $7 million for Army Emergency Relief.

Kids and Christmas

Of course, theaters continued their annual tradition of taking care of the young ones at Christmas. In addition to things like parties, free screenings in exchange for canned goods and visits from Santa, the marquee event each year during World War II was Wilmington's "Toy for Every Child" campaign. After a successful 1941 campaign, once the war was fully on, the program struggled.

The 1942 campaign, with its slogan "Share Your Toys," saw numbers down. Every child was still taken care of, but analysis of the event determined that donations of metal toys (bikes, wagons and the like), normally the program's biggest category, were down sharply. The thinking was that the drop was due to scrap drives claiming the old toys that in previous years would have gone to the Christmas campaign.

Theaters adapted and in 1943 adopted a new slogan: "New Toys for Every Child." With the disappearance of so many old toys for scrap drives, theaters asked the public for new toys or for cash to buy new

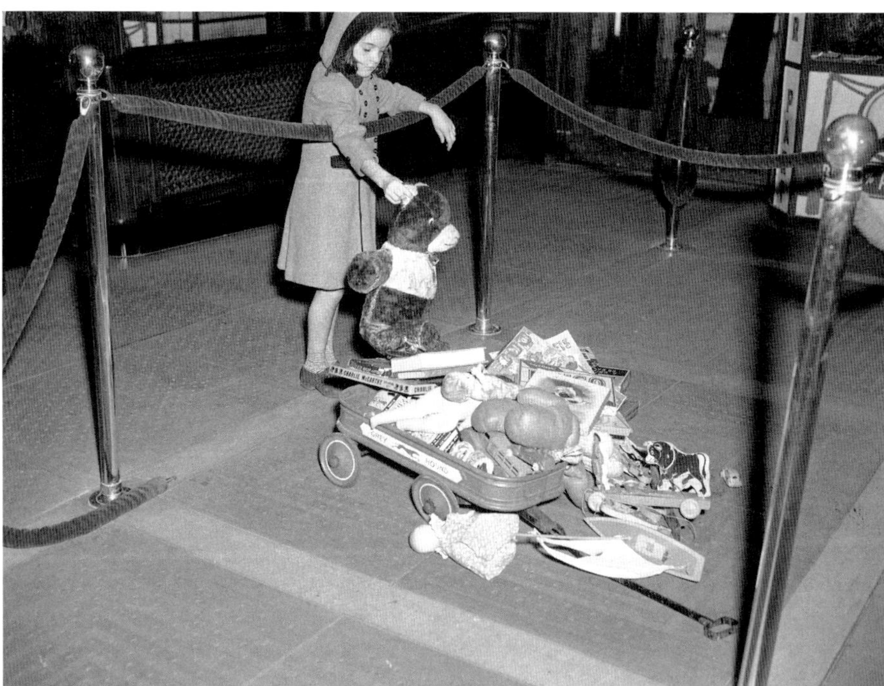

A child donates toys at an unknown Wilmington theater for one of the city's "Toys for Every Child" campaigns (undated). *Delaware Public Archives.*

toys. The goal was met, but again it was a struggle. (A quick pause to say 1943 was also the year theaters played the Bing Crosby short *Now, About Christmas* to raise awareness of the Christmas Seals campaign being run by the National Tuberculosis Association, creating greater "demand" for holiday donations.)

"Toys for Wilmington's Hospitalized Children" was the phrase of 1944, and then "Toys for Every Needy Child" in 1945. In both years, late donations barely saved the day. It's easy to understand why, though. So many people were already giving so much in so many areas, it's possible "giving burnout" was a factor.

THE ENTERTAINMENT

Putting on a Show Over Here Before Shipping Off Over There

Before the advent of motion pictures, theaters offered only live entertainment, so it stands to reason that all movie theaters have in their DNA this potential to offer more than just movies. While perhaps not as much in the multiplex era, the capacity for live presentations was quite high in the World War II era, as theaters around the state at that time were either old enough to have been originally built for live entertainment and then modified for movies, or they were built for movies but designed to accommodate live presentations as well. Plays, concerts, beauty pageants and other events were a staple at these places during this time. This was especially true at the military bases, which played host to routine USO Camp shows. And when those road shows weren't in town, the bases had their own in-house entertainment that also took their show on the road.

The Bands of the New Castle Army Air Base

Jive Bombers: The New Castle Army Air Base had four bands in its five-year history. The Jive Bombers were first and, by all accounts, the most popular band at the base and around the state.

Formed in December 1942 with three members, the Jive Bombers were a swing band that was a subset of the NCAAB 392nd Detachment

The USO show *Come What May* plays at the New Castle Army Air Base in what is likely the base theater (1944). *Delaware Public Archives.*

Band. They played on-base gigs in their early days and bolstered their roster to thirteen, which included prewar members of big bands and college bands. In July 1943, they made their very public debut at the dedication of the Delaware War Bond Center in the Delaware Power & Light Building in Wilmington.

The rest must have been a blur, because even though military regulations limited their appearances to military and war loan functions, there were so many of those things going on at any given time, the Jive Bombers—who were credited with increasing bond sales at events—were in constant demand.

In addition to numerous appearances at the Delaware War Bond Center, the Jive Bombers played street dances (outside the War Bond Center), the first of which saw three thousand people dancing among the seven to eight thousand milling about; a WAC recruiting event in March 1944; and meetings at the Queen Theatre, where city retailers prepared for the Third, Fourth, Fifth and Sixth War Loan Drives.

Above: The Jive Bombers of the New Castle Army Air Base play a gig at the Delaware War Bond Center in Wilmington (circa 1943). *Delaware Public Archives.*

Left: The Jive Bombers of the New Castle Army Air Base play a Third War Loan Drive gig (circa September 1943). *Delaware Public Archives.*

Opposite: Actor Dean Jagger appears with the Jive Bombers at the opening of the War Bond Center at the Delaware Power & Light building in Wilmington on July 2, 1943. *Delaware Public Archives.*

The Jive Bombers not only helped raise money for the war but also helped their fellow veterans with gigs like the October 1943 Delaware Soldiers Christmas Committee dance at Wilmington's Armory; a November 1943 event at the U.S. Veterans Hospital (Perry Point, Maryland); the March 1944 conference to prepare for the opening of the Red Cross Veterans Clearing Bureau; and the October 1944 Delaware Conference on Employment of Veterans, held at the Hotel DuPont.

When not doing all of that, they were helping fellow entertainers, like the times they supplied the music for their fellow base members who put on the *Strictly G.I.* shows (see later in this chapter), and for the USO's December 1943 *Fancy That* Camp Show.

No gig was too obscure for the Jive Bombers, either. In February 1944 alone, they played a war bond fashion show at the Playhouse, a war loan sports carnival at the Amory and a dance for French sailors at the YMCA.

No gig was too small, either. In May 1944, they played a war bond fashion show at Ursuline Academy; the month prior, only a vocalist and pianist were required for a stockholders' meeting of the Retail Grocers Exchange held in the Hotel DuPont (with the military providing speakers from several branches as well); and in October 1944 they performed for a war fund drive jitterbug contest at the Armory.

The Jive Bombers of the New Castle Army Air Base (June 1944). *Delaware Public Archives.*

Did I mention this was on top of two dances a week at the base?

It's no wonder they found themselves with a following, including a fan club. As Jive Bombers Jive Club president Jenny Speakman put it in a letter to the Wilmington Junior Chamber of Commerce (sponsor of the street dances), "This band is very popular with the younger set of boys and girls in Wilmington."

But we were still at war, and the Jive Bombers were still in the service, so in December 1944, just seventeen months after the Jive Bombers' public debut, the 392nd Detachment Band (which had since been renamed the 692nd AAF Band) was deployed overseas, and the Jive Bombers went with them, leaving an incredible legacy in a very short period of time.

Ad Liberators: The 692nd AAF Band from which the Jive Bombers were formed had such a deep bench, it formed the Ad Liberators in October 1943. The difference between the two bands was probably best described by William P. Frank in his *Evening Journal* column "The Man About Town," in which he assessed the Jive Bombers as being the "hot orchestra" while the Ad Liberators "give out sweet music."

Private First Class Eddie Schwatlo (*standing, right*) leads the Ad Liberators of the New Castle Army Air Base (1944). *Delaware Public Archives.*

The Ad Liberators played gigs similar to the Jive Bombers (although fewer, it seems, based on news reports), including on-base events and events at the Delaware War Bond Center. Their biggest event appears to have been the first Book and Authors Rally at the Playhouse in June 1944. But, when it was time for the 692nd AAF Band to head overseas, the Ad Liberators, like the Jive Bombers, went with their unit.

SKYMEISTERS: With the Jive Bombers and the Ad Liberators deployed to Europe, there was large hole in the live band landscape at NCAAB. That hole was filled by the Skymeisters. A lot of the gigs they played were base-specific, like parties, dances and ceremonies, and of course they played the obligatory retailer meeting at the Queen in May 1945, but from time to time they got the kind of flashier gigs their predecessors were known to play. The band played the following gigs in May 1945 alone: the Parade of Stars at the Armory; an all-high school bond dance, also at the Armory, with well-known intermission acts and appearances by actor/composer Buddy Pepper and announcer Lew Lowry; and an NCO club dedication, with announcer Lew Lowry and the Chord Busters Quartet. The one thing that set them apart from the Jive Bombers and Ad Liberators? The Skymeisters had WACs on vocals.

Crew Chiefs: Just as the Jive Bombers had the Ad Liberators, the Skymeisters had the Crew Chiefs, although news reports say the Skymeisters played the "dreamy stuff" while the Crew Chiefs played "hot." The band was a very late entry at the NCAAB, but they partnered with the Skymeisters at the May 1945 all-high school dance at the Armory.

The Bands of Fort Miles, Dover Army Air Base/ Air Field and Fort DuPont

Harbor Defense Band: The most obvious, and arguably the most significant, contribution the Harbor Defense Band of Fort Miles made to World War II entertainment in Delaware was providing music for the Fort Miles Players and their successful run of shows (see later in this chapter). But the Harbor Defense Band was not just some acting troupe's house band; they contributed plenty on their own.

Unlike the bands in New Castle, which had their own names and styles, the Harbor Defense Band was, for all intents and purposes, two bands with one name, giving them a more consistent "brand" as any gig they played was as the Harbor Defense Band, not Band A and Band B. Those shared gigs included numerous dances on- and off-base, as well as in parades for patriotic holidays like Memorial Day in Delaware City and Independence Day in Lewes; an Armistice Day gig at their own base's theater; and a bond rally for the Lewes Chamber of Commerce. All of those events were in 1942. And they weren't limited to the big-band sound of the era or the military-style music reserved for parades and formal military functions. On Good Friday in 1943, they played a concert of sacred music.

But perhaps their biggest (non-Players) appearance was at Milford's New Plaza Theatre in October 1943, where they played, as something of an opening act, in advance of the sold-out bond screening of *This Is the Army*. One other fun event they played was something of a battle of the bands, where the band's two individual groups set up on opposite sides of the base rec hall and alternated tunes for their hundreds of guests.

The Sandunaires and Their Miles of Melody: Not unlike the circumstance in New Castle, military requirements took the Harbor Defense Band away from Fort Miles, leaving the base with an all-new band in April 1944. The band had no name, so it held a contest, and this was the winner.

Fort Miles's own the Sandunaires and Their Miles of Melody (circa 1944). *Delaware Public Archives.*

The Fort DuPont Band (circa 1944). *Delaware Public Archives.*

The name is a heavy play on the words "sand dunes" (of Lewes and the neighboring beaches), "Miles" (for the Fort) and "melody" (for song). The band played weekly dances for enlisted men, biweekly dances for officers, one-off dances in and around the base as occasions called and of course at bond-selling events. One notable and unique appearance was the start of an ongoing monthly tradition: a party for the civilian employees of the base for "a remarkable record of efficiency in their wartime duties."*

DOVER THUNDERBOLTS: In addition to traditional base play, the Dover Thunderbolts of the Dover Army Air Base/Air Field played an eight-hundred-person block dance in Smyrna in August 1944, and they were part of a "Bond Caravan" for the Sixth War Loan Drive that began in Seaford and toured Kent and Sussex Counties.

FORT DUPONT BAND: Originally called the First Engineers Band (prewar) and, like its brother bands around the state, on hand to play base-traditional gigs, one of the Fort DuPont Band's most notable appearances was playing a reception in Wilmington that honored Delaware World War II hero Lieutenant George S. Welch.

FORT DUPONT CONTINENTALS: Only two events mention this band by name, both in February 1944, but they were key events. During the Fourth War Loan Drive, the Continentals were tapped to play a sports carnival held at Wilmington's Armory (an event they shared with the Jive Bombers—one that drew 1,500 people and raised $403,000). They were also part of the vaudeville portion of the *Riding High* bond premiere screening at the Warner Theatre.

THE FORT MILES PLAYERS

For all intents and purposes, this was a theater troupe consisting entirely of servicemen stationed at Fort Miles, the original iteration of which was led by Privates David Fitzgibbon and Stanley Ross, themselves no strangers to the prewar spotlight. Fitzgibbon was described by local papers as a "musical comedy dancing star and choreographer," and a young one at that, with a career that began when he was fifteen and took him from the States to England to Copenhagen and back to the States. Ross had his own band that played at the Manhattan Room of the Hotel New Yorker. But it's important to note that all the men in the Players were soldiers first—they had regular

---

* *Morning News* (Wilmington, DE), September 14, 1944.

Privates John Fox and Leo Monk, both members of the Fort Miles Players, review a poster promoting their musical revue, "Here We Go," being presented at Wilmington's Playhouse on December 1, 1942. *Delaware Public Archives.*

on-base duties and put together the shows, from conception to production, on their own time.

Here We Go: This first production from the Fort Miles Players—who hadn't even been named as such yet—was an all-soldier twelve-act satirical musical revue about a group of soldiers on leave in New York City. Both the book and music were original and written by Fort Miles servicemen, with a cast of seventeen soldiers and an orchestra of eighteen more (the Harbor Defense Band).

After playing to servicemen at several bases in Delaware and New Jersey beginning in September 1942, and after a mid-November performance at Seaford's Layton Theatre, the military showmen loaded up two trucks and made their way north from Lewes to Wilmington, where they were booked for a one-night performance at the Playhouse. The standing-room-only crowd loved the show, which the next day's edition of the *Wilmington Morning News* called "a rollicking collection of vaudeville that kept its audience laughing and applauding." It was reported that after the show, the men went to the Hotel DuPont Grille, where the Defense Band took over for the orchestra and played even hotter than they had in the show.

The night raised $1,100 for a good cause: the Delaware Red Cross Camp and Hospital Council, which would also see proceeds from the troupe's final performance of the show at Dover's Capitol Theatre in mid-December.

Fun's a Flyin': In February 1943, this second show from the Fort Miles Players was such a hit, it went on a tour of New Jersey army camps after playing in Lewes, Georgetown, and Milford. What made the production special—beyond its sixteen acts—was the inclusion of the hit song "Harbor Defense of the Delaware March"; that tune had been penned by Fort Miles sergeant technicians Jesse Berkman and Mark Laub, formerly of Fort DuPont.

Dog Tags of 1943: Another original musical written by members of the Fort Miles Players was a show-within-a-show satire about a camp theater troupe being quarantined with mumps on the eve of performing for a distinguished audience and how up-and-comers needed to save the day. The play had a March preview performance at the Rehoboth Fire Hall before opening to positive reviews at the Fort Miles Theatre and hitting the road to perform for outlying camps. Fitzgibbon (now a corporal), who appeared in and directed the show, was deemed the "Fred Astaire of Fort Miles"* for his fancy footwork.

On the Cuff: In May 1943, this fourth show put on by the Players came with a unique twist: each night would offer surprises that required audience participation. Skits included a mock ballet and a "G.I. Fashion Show." Renowned jazz musician Ted Lewis ("Is Everybody Happy?"), recent to Fort Miles, joined the cast; the Harbor Defense Band provided tunes; and again the post theater was the place to be to see the show.

Passing the Buck: The Players' fifth entry in their growing résumé was a late June/early July series of comedy sketches structured to look like the

---

* *Delaware Wave*, January 21, 2020.

Three Fort Miles Players perform "Why Did I Join the WAACs" in *Dog Tags of 1943* (*left to right*): Private First Class Craig Edwards, Private Paul Millman and Corporal Charlie Lewis. The show was performed at the Fort Miles Theatre in March 1943. *Delaware Public Archives.*

players were plucked from the audience. The production, performed at the Fort Miles Theatre, again included musical accompaniment from the Harbor Defense Band.

Of G.I. Sing: In September 1943, the Players performed a revue that curiously got almost no press attention; it's curious because their other performances—even the lesser-known ones—received coverage ranging from decent to heavy. The revue was performed at the post theater, seemingly one time.

Rollin' Abroad: One quick but busy year after their smash debut *Here We Go*, the Players' seventh, and most ambitious, effort yet would take them back to not only Wilmington but also a lot of other stops around the state.

Again written entirely by Fort Miles servicemen, *Rollin' Abroad* was a musical satire directed at officers and regulations, first with a new soldier's early experiences in the army and then soldiers' travels abroad. With a cast and orchestra totaling sixty strong (almost double their first outing), the show had its well-received November 24 premiere in the Lewes High School auditorium for a civilian crowd. That was the first of eight shows in ten nights for the Players and the band. After Lewes High, they played at Fort Miles, the Rehoboth School auditorium, Fort DuPont, the Georgetown School auditorium, the Layton and Capitol theaters and the New Castle Army Air Base—all as tune-ups to their highly anticipated two-night stint at Wilmington's Playhouse.

Those Playhouse shows, the first of which was part of the December 7 Delaware Day Observance, met with good reviews, although anecdotally the responses leaned toward this production being a little more pretentious than *Here We Go*. Still, the cause was good (again the Red Cross Camp and Hospital Council), bonds and stamps were sold in the lobby and the trip afforded some of the band members to play a side gig at the Delaware War Bond Center while they were in town. A stop at Dover Army Air Base on the way south was what appeared to be their final show.

ONE TOUCH OF GENIUS: The Fort Miles Players don't appear in news items again until late 1945, when they were touted as having been "revived." (I have to wonder if the troupe followed a similar path as the Jive Bombers

The Fort Miles Players rehearse *Rollin' Abroad* in late 1943. *Delaware Public Archives.*

and others that found themselves deployed.) The revived Players closed out the year with this musical revue spoof of *One Touch of Venus*. The performances—the original in October and a command performance in November—were held for servicemen and civilians alike at the post theater. Making the production unique was the inclusion of a SPAR in the cast. Marjorie Grenier, stationed in Bethany Beach, joined the traditionally male-only Fort Miles Players for these productions.

Other Live Shows and Entertainments

The lads at Fort Miles weren't the only game in the state.

The Technicolor Revue: Getting in on the live performance action in February 1942, the Special Services Office of Fort DuPont produced *The Technicolor Revue*, which featured in its cast members of the First Chemical Company, an organization of all-Black troops.

They Can't Do That to Us: In March 1942, Fort DuPont's Special Services delivered again, this time with a show of their own. In addition to performing for their own men, they also traveled to Fort Miles to perform for the men of that base. Costumes were made by the Red Cross.

Room Service: Another month and another show for Fort DuPont, this one furnished in April 1942 by the II Corps Area Theatre Section. The play featured servicemen with Broadway experience, as well as a pair of actual actresses (not soldiers in drag), also with Broadway experience.

Even Stephen: In something of a twist, the Fort Miles Theatre was the site of this three-act play put on by students from Rehoboth High School in March 1943. Apparently, someone from the base saw the show at the high school and thought the men stationed at Fort Miles would enjoy it, and they did. The theater was sold out on very short notice.

Strictly G.I.: The all-soldier show *Strictly G.I.*, a collection of skits and songs of both local and army origin, was presented in the New Castle Army Air Base rec hall in October 1943. The cast consisted of base personnel and one WAC from Wilmington, with music provided by the Jive Bombers. It was so well-received, a version of it was performed in November for the American Legion Armistice Day program in Kennett Square, Pennsylvania.

The Army Play by Play: Produced by Uncle Sam in 1943, following the wild success of *This Is the Army* the previous year (a live show that did not make it to Delaware), *The Army Play by Play* actually began as a contest for servicemen to write and submit one-act plays that could be produced locally at bases around the world. The best five plays chosen were incorporated into what became this larger show, where the plays were put on and separated by musical numbers, comedy, dancing and other vaudevillian entertainment. The first production was supposed to be a one-time-only presentation in New York City. After earning over $100,000 and an on-stage plea from Mayor Fiorella LaGuardia (alongside guests Eleanor Roosevelt and the Duke and Duchess of Windsor) for more performances, the play returned for a brief NYC run, followed by a tour. Wilmington's Playhouse was one of those stops for a three-night engagement in mid-October; proceeds benefited Army Emergency Relief.

Like the shows put on by the boys from Fort Miles, this was an all-soldier production, but with eighty men in the cast and twenty-five in the pit. The local news cited that this was the "first touring soldier show to play Wilmington," which suggests since the Fort Miles Players were based in Delaware, their state tour didn't really count as a tour.

The five one-act plays, set in army barracks, the hull of a German submarine, a washroom, a shelter behind enemy lines and a receiving station warehouse, were all received well, as was the overall show, which one critic called "clever, spirited, and swift-moving."

Oh, and one of the cast members was Jules Munshin, who, after the war, would go on to appear in several films, including *On the Town* with Frank Sinatra and Gene Kelly.

DAAFie Delights: In August 1944, soldiers from Dover Army Air Field and hostesses from the Dover USO joined forces to put on the musical comedy revue *DAAFie Delights* at the Dover High School auditorium. Admission was free, and music was provided by the Dover Thunderbolts.

Stage Door Canteen Night: The first Stage Door Canteen, located in New York's theater district, opened in March 1942. It offered servicemen free entertainment, food, nonalcoholic drinks and even the chance to cross paths with the likes of Marlene Dietrich, Bette Davis and Lauren Bacall. It was a massive success, and over the course of the war, other Canteens opened in eight major cities around the country, as well as in London and Paris. It is estimated eleven million servicemen were entertained and fed during that time.

There was no Canteen in Delaware, but that didn't stop the New Castle Army Air Base from creating its own, at least for one night. On May 30, 1945, in celebration of the Second Ferrying Group's third anniversary and the Air Transport Command's fourth anniversary, the gymnasium at New Castle Army Air Base was converted to look like New York's Stage Door Canteen, but it did not stop at the aesthetic.

The Dover Army Air Base's Paul Costello, Joseph McPhieters and Albert Rodman as "The Andrews Sisters" in the musical comedy revue *DAAFie Delights* (1944). *Delaware Public Archives.*

In addition to the 150 hostesses brought in from the Philadelphia Stage Door Canteen, event organizers stocked the place with a list of entertainment to treat the two thousand–plus in attendance:

Corporal Johnny Messner and his twenty-piece orchestra
Metropolitan Opera star Helen Jepson
Radio and screen singer James Melton

The Mitchell Ayres Orchestra
Comedian Jackie Kelk
Popular vocal quartet The Merry Macs
Jean Tighe, soloist formerly of the Guy Lombardo Orchestra
Singer Ann Francine of New York's Versailles Club
Mike Chimes, harmonica player
Pat Flowers, boogie-woogie pianist and protégé of the late Fats Waller
Patsy Garrett, singer
Private First Class Omer Pelletier and his dog Snooks, whose act wowed them at Radio City Music Hall
Fourteen Harry Conover Models

The night also featured messages of congratulations from President Harry Truman, General George Marshall and other top brass. The final highlight of the night was the selection of "Miss Eileen of the New Castle Army Air Base," an honor bestowed on Marie Pounds of Upper Darby in Delaware County, Pennsylvania, who was one of the Philadelphia Canteen hostesses in attendance.

THE MOVIES

Premieres and Propaganda at 24fps

There were a lot of movies shown for a lot of reasons in Delaware during World War II, with many of them—at least in the context of this book—associated with big events. But what about the notable movies that *weren't* shown for loan drives or scrap collection or Christmas fun or just for free? And I say "notable" because there were tens of thousands of screenings at all Delaware theaters during the World War II era, and it would be impossible (fun, but impossible) to try to capture and record all of them.

During my research for this book, I came across a lot of interesting movies that were shown around the state for various reasons but didn't fit neatly into other chapters. I still thought they deserved a mention, so I gave them a chapter of their own.

Newsreels

These short, documentary-style films were shown in theaters as part of larger entertainment packages that may have included shorts, cartoons and a feature or two. Newsreels shown during World War II offered current events and other news, with a lot of footage from the war. Newsreel "brands" included Fox Movietone News, Hearst Metrotone News, Paramount News, Pathé News and Universal Newsreel.

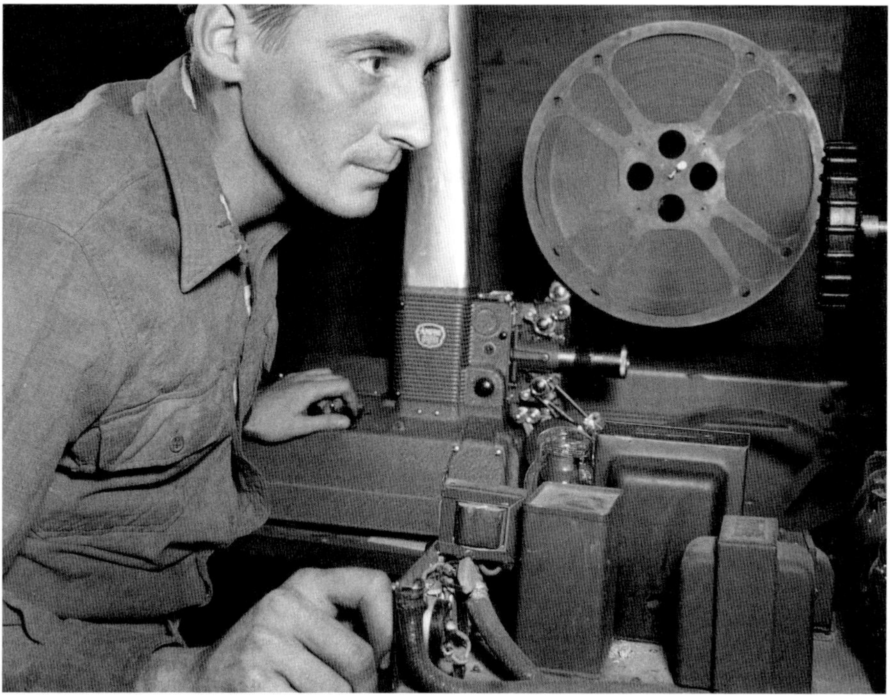

U.S. Army sergeant Harvey Tyre, of Wilmington, was a projectionist at the Allied Forces Headquarters in the Mediterranean theater (undated). *Delaware Public Archives.*

One other newsreel entry was Time Inc.'s *The March of Time* series. While offering news and other information, *The March of Time* shorts (most in the ten- to twenty-minute range) also included dramatizations, and they were regularly advertised when they played. One notable screening was their first feature-length entry, *The Ramparts We Watch*, at the Aldine in September 1940. Using World War I as its history lesson, the film offers the message that just because there is a war in Europe that has no direct effect on the country, Americans should still be prepared.

Another notable screening was a short shown at the Rialto in June 1943—*Show-Business at War*—that covers Hollywood's efforts to support the war. It's an information-packed and entertaining seventeen-minute film, with far too much in it to summarize here, although I will say I was surprised they mentioned Carole Lombard's death flying home from a bond drive.

As a curious aside, there are several stories during the war about Delaware theatergoers seeing loved ones in newsreels on-screen, including one story about the war wife who thought she saw her husband in one reel at the Warner. She sat through the same picture three times to be triply sure, then returned the next day with a friend to confirm it. Indeed it was her husband, who was part of a tank destroyer battalion in Luxembourg. Warner Theatre manager Lewis Black gave her a strip of the film containing her husband's picture.

Propaganda Pictures

Britannica.com describes *propaganda* as "the more or less systematic effort to manipulate other people's beliefs, attitudes, or actions by means of symbols (words, gestures, banners, monuments, music, clothing, insignia, hairstyles, designs on coins and postage stamps, and so forth)."

There was plenty of that in America during World War II—in newspapers, on the radio, on posters and most certainly on film, where at any time a propagandic message could be found in any random moving picture that any random theater was screening. That propaganda was used isn't to say most Americans needed their beliefs changed, but the country certainly benefited from having positive patriotic notions routinely reinforced. While the intent and execution of the use of propaganda within the framework of America's involvement in World War II can be debated, there is no denying it was effective, particularly on the silver screen.

Part I—The Shorts: Short films were effective tools of propaganda, as their efficient length and topic specificity gave them a lot of punch and made quick work of getting their messages across—messages that included celebrating the country, supporting the military, championing a cause, making a sacrifice or disparaging the enemy.

Propaganda on film began before Pearl Harbor, and it was not limited to theaters. Part of a March 1941 junior high assembly at the A.I. DuPont School included the screening of *Aluminum*, a ten-minute film produced by the Office of Emergency Management Film Unit. The middle of the short is as dry as a junior high physical science lecture—the life cycle of aluminum, from the mining of its ore to the creation of its shiny, sheeted final state. But the short is bookended by opening images and narration of Nazis invading Europe (and affecting that continent's aluminum supply) and closing images and narration of how all this aluminum we produce will be used to manufacture American war planes.

Back in theaters, in September and October of that same year, the Loew's Aldine, Arcadia and Savoy all screened *Defense for America*, a short

Left: This is a poster promoting a 1942 documentary short film about the need for scrap metal. *National Archives and Records Administration.*

Right: This generic poster could have been used (and reused) to promote any defense film screenings (undated). *National Archives and Records Administration.*

film produced by the National Association of Manufacturers that takes the viewer inside defense plants during periods of operation to show how production lines create things like tanks, bombers and other war materiel.

In January 1942, less than six weeks after Pearl Harbor, the Loew's Aldine screened MGM's *Main Street on the March*, an incredibly effective twenty-minute film that opens in a town that could be any town in America and shows how that town, which didn't have a care in the world, gradually transforms as the prospect of the United States going war evolves from unlikely (when many people dismissed Germany's invasion of Poland as a European concern only), to possible (when Germany invaded Holland in 1940), to inevitable (Pearl Harbor). The film adeptly illustrates how the country, after a rousing speech from President Roosevelt, went from being militarily underprepared to being a powerhouse, thanks in part to the many sacrifices made by people in towns all around the country. It is no surprise the film went on to win the Oscar for Best Short Subject (two-reel).

In the spring of 1942, the Queen, Arcadia and Savoy screened *American Anniversary*, a tale about an immigrant celebrating his twentieth year as a citizen of this country. Later that year, the same trio of Wilmington theaters screened *Ring of Steel*, a Spencer Tracy–narrated tribute to the American soldier. Another military-themed short narrated by a Hollywood luminary played at the Rialto in June 1943: *Wings Up*, a short about Officers Candidate School of the Army Air Forces, was narrated by Clark Gable and also featured William Holden as himself.

In March 1944, the Warner Theatre hosted the Delaware Safety Council, which screened several shorts: *The Case of the Tremendous Trifle*, which takes viewers through the planning of a bombing of a German ball-bearing plant (including the interrogation of Germans for intel); *Film Communique #5*, which focuses on P-47s; *Life Line*, about getting medical supplies to the front; and *They Deliver the Goods*, about getting other war materiel to the front.

In the last year of the war, familiar Wilmington theaters the Loew's Aldine, Queen, Rialto and Warner screened *Two Down and One to Go*, a Frank Capra–directed thirty-minute short that uses a combination of animated graphics and actual war footage to recap America's strategy on beating Italy and Germany, reminding everyone we still had Japan to beat.

Further to Frank Capra's work on war-related short films, I confirmed the first installment of his well-known documentary series, *Why We Fight*, did screen at the Warner in June 1943. I found no evidence the other six installments played anywhere in Delaware, but I suspect they did and simply weren't advertised. All seven installments, in release order, are *Prelude to War* (1942), *The Nazis Strike* (1943), *Divide and Conquer* (1943), *The Battle of Britain* (1943), *The Battle of Russia* (1943), *The Battle of China* (1944) and *War Comes to America* (1945).

PART II—THE CARTOONS: As was the case with feature films and live-action shorts, animated shorts—cartoons—evolved to align with the topics and sentiments of the day. Proof of that evolution is found in raw numbers. In 1939, of the 158 cartoon shorts to be released theatrically from seven major studios (Columbia, Disney, MGM, Paramount, 20th Century Fox, Universal and Warner Bros.), only 4 shorts were war-related. Two years later, 26 of 163 cartoon shorts were about the war. And in 1943, the ratio peaked at 81 war-related cartoons against 120 released. Over the course of the war, the totals are telling: 477 cartoon shorts were released, and of them, 225—almost half—were somehow war-related.

And like their feature-length and live-action-short counterparts, cartoons were used as propaganda, leveraging the popularity of characters ranging

from Andy Panda to Woody Woodpecker and all the popular ones in between—Donald Duck, Bugs Bunny, Tom and Jerry, and even Popeye (think about it, *he was already a sailor*)—to address, either directly or by way of references of varying subtlety, topics including bonds, the draft, Hitler, Mussolini, MacArthur, FDR (Eleanor too!), Pearl Harbor and many others.

But Popeye and Bugs and Company weren't the only animated characters to hit screens. Two collections of animated shorts were produced specifically for the military and played only on bases and other military locations: *Mr. Hook* and *Private Snafu*. The entries for the former, produced circa 1944–45 by Warner Bros. for the U.S. Navy, number in the single digits and focus on bonds. The latter, with over two dozen entries mostly produced by Warner Bros. circa 1943–45, were created mostly by people whose names are synonymous with Looney Tunes: directors Chuck Jones, Friz Freleng and Frank Tashlin; composer Carl W. Stalling; and voice actor Mel Blanc. Also responsible for writing many of these two-to-five-minute Private Snafu shorts were Theodore Geisel (aka Dr. Suess) and his protégé Phil Eastman. The Snafu shorts were humorous looks at military life but with important messages regarding things like health, secrecy, military protocol and more. They were also racy!

Despite the popularity of the hundreds of commercially released cartoons, and despite how well-recorded they are elsewhere, the challenge of documenting them here is knowing when and where they played in Delaware, as they weren't advertised the way features were. If mentioned

Opposite, left: Not only does eating spinach make Popeye strong, it gives him portmanteau skills (undated). *National Archives and Records Administration.*

Opposite, right: Even Snuffy Smith wants a piece of the action (undated). *National Archives and Records Administration.*

Left: Don't make Li'l Abner angry. You won't like him when he's angry (undated). *National Archives and Records Administration.*

in advertising at all, cartoons were promoted by theaters based on main characters, not titles (such as "A New Donald Duck Cartoon").

But the Park Theatre and Pike Theatre shared titles in some of their ads. In late December 1945, the Park screened both *Commando Duck* (featuring Donald Duck) and *Bugs Bunny Nips the Nips*. Among other things, both shorts are anti-Japan and feature disparaging caricatures. The Pike, in July 1944, showed *Jasper Goes Fishing*, a George Pal–directed "Puppetoon" with a pro-military theme; in January 1945, the theater played the Goofy-starring *Victory Vehicles*, about resource shortages; and in June 1945, it showed Bugs Bunny in *Herr Meets Hare*, an anti-Germany, pro-military cartoon.

(Actual) War Pictures

Beyond Hollywood's dramatization of war in its fictional films, there were films produced that were heavier in content and starker in visuals—films that were real.

In January 1942, the Ace Theatre screened *Target for Tonight*, a docudrama made in England about a bombing mission in Germany, starring actual RAF crew members. In September of that same year, the Rialto and the Warner screened *The Battle of Midway*, the John Ford–directed documentary about the famed battle in which the U.S. Navy thwarted Japan's efforts to

Combat America (1945), a documentary starring and produced by Clark Gable, recounts experiences of the U.S. Army Air Forces 351st Bombardment Group. The author could not confirm that this screened in Delaware. *National Archives and Records Administration.*

capture Midway Island; the film is composed of actual combat footage shot by Ford and his crew.

The Memphis Belle: A Story of a Flying Fortress screened at the Loew's Aldine in April 1944. The film is a documentary of the first B-17 bomber to complete twenty-five missions, and it features actual combat footage shot by a crew led by director William Wyler. In June 1944, nine Wilmington theaters screened D-Day Invasion Pictures featuring actual footage from D-Day. And in 1945, the New Castle Army Air Base (at an August open house) showed the Ronald Reagan–narrated *Target Tokyo*, about the first bombing mission of Tokyo by B-29s, while in September the Queen screened *The True Glory*, a feature-length documentary about the Allied invasion of Europe, compiled from footage shot by 1,400 cameramen.

There was even a war bond premiere of a documentary. In March 1945, the Rialto sold bonds as tickets for a screening of *The Fighting Lady*, a doc using actual footage to provide audiences with a look at aircraft carrier combat operations during the war.

Recruiting Films

In addition to the WAAC/WAC and AWVS recruiting films mentioned in "The Bombshells: WAACs, WAVES, WASPs, and Other World War Women," other organizations used movies to recruit new members. In July 1940, the navy screened a recruiting film at the Warner. In April 1942, the film *Soldiers of the Sea* was screened outside of the Wilmington Public Building as part of a recruiting effort by the Marines. In June 1944, the Rialto screened *Reward Unlimited* to help recruit ladies into the U.S. Cadet Nurse Corps. And three months later, the WAVES were recruiting at the Queen with screenings of *Report to Judy*.

Training Films

There was no YouTube during World War II, so education by way of visualization needed to be screened full-size. If you wanted to learn about map reading or the tactical employment of a 155mm howitzer, the theater at Fort DuPont was the place to be in March 1941. Proper disposal of incendiary devices was covered in *Fighting the Fire Bomb* at the Pike Theatre in 1942. And Red Cross first-aid training films were screened at Fort DuPont in 1943.

The Greats

Most of the movies in this chapter are doing work—training or recruiting or reporting or propagandizing. But there were a lot of films released during America's involvement in the war that were just plain great. Yes, they may have had propagandic themes, but a lot of films had those and only a small percentage have withstood the test of time. Below are the seven films released in the United States and screened in Wilmington between 1942 and 1945 that have been given four stars by one of the greatest film critics of all time, the late Roger Ebert, and when/where they played.

Casablanca
Michael Curtiz, 1942
February 4, 1943 | Warner Theatre

Cat People
Jacques Tourneur, 1942
April 25, 1943 | Grand Theatre

Double Indemnity
Billy Wilder, 1944
August 3, 1944 | Warner Theatre

Laura
Otto Preminger, 1944
November 21, 1944 | Rialto Theatre

The Life and Death of Colonel Blimp
Michael Powell and Emeric Pressburger, 1943
October 11, 1945 | Loew's Aldine

Shadow of a Doubt
Alfred Hitchcock, 1943
April 2, 1943 | Queen Theatre

Yankee Doodle Dandy
Michael Curtiz, 1942
September 3, 1942 | Warner Theatre

THE STARS

Celebrity Cameos in the First State

Delaware has been no stranger to hosting the famous. From the early 1900s, celebrities from Annie Oakley and Buffalo Bill Cody to Louis Armstrong and Enrico Caruso entertained theatergoers around the state. Even three of the Warner brothers themselves—Harry, Albert and Jack—have been to the First State (although their visit was not to entertain but to stave off a hostile takeover of the studio, but still).

The Playhouse has been the place to be to see those who are the type to be seen, as well-known actors and actresses have graced its stage in myriad live productions over the years. In the World War II era, the theater saw performances from the likes of:

Brian Aherne	*The French Touch* (1945)
Tallulah Bankhead	*Foolish Notion* (1945)
Ethel Barrymore	*The Corn Is Green* (1943 and 1944), *Embezzled Heaven* (1944)
Constance Bennett	*Easy Virtue* (1939)
Billie Burke	*Mrs. January and Mrs. Ex* (1944)
Leo G. Carroll	*The Late George Apley* (1944)
Arlene Francis	*The French Touch* (1945)
Dorothy Gish	*The Magnificent Yankee* (1945)
Katharine Hepburn	*Without Love* (1942)

Miriam Hopkins	*The Perfect Marriage* (1944)
Dean Jagger	*Yankee Point* (1942)
Boris Karloff	*Arsenic and Old Lace* (twice in 1943)
Gene Lockhart	*Happily Ever After* (1945)
Bela Lugosi	*Arsenic and Old Lace* (1944)
Raymond Massey	*Lincoln: The War Years* (1941)
ZaSu Pitts	*Her First Murder!* (1942)
Sylvia Sidney	*Jane Eyre* (1944)
Gloria Swanson	*Three Curtains* (1942)
Dickie Van Patten	*Decision* (1944)
Erich von Stroheim	*Arsenic and Old Lace* (1941)
Gloria Warren	*What's Up* (1943)
Roland Young	*Another Love Story* (1943)

Actor Robert Ryan at the Robin Hood Theatre (1941). *Delaware Public Archives.*

The Robin Hood Theatre hosted its share of stars as well. From the theater's beginnings and over the course of World War II (and into the 1960s), its focus was on live performances, but some of those players came with Hollywood bona fides. Lila Lee had nearly one hundred film credits between her first appearance in the silent era in *The Cruise of the Make-Believes* (1918, at age seventeen) and her 1941 appearance at the Robin Hood in the play *Invitation to Murder*. Also in that play was future Oscar nominee Robert Ryan, who was just cutting his teeth in Hollywood. In 1942, Miriam Battista, with almost two dozen (credited and uncredited) films to her name, starred in *The Barker*. Loring Smith, who was also just getting started in Hollywood, was a member of the Robin Hood's summer troupe in 1942. Also appearing on stage in 1942 were experienced screen actors Morgan Farley and Robert Allen.

But it was during the World War II era that Delaware saw its share of celebrities come to town(s) to raise money, please crowds, entertain troops—and in some cases serve their country.

THE MONEY RAISERS

> *Instantly the United States was drawn into the war, Hollywood leaders realized that there soon would be an avalanche of requests for "free talent." Such an avalanche was inevitable, because America has learned that Hollywood's famous personalities are super-salesmen, whether they are selling an attitude, a patriotic cause or war bonds. It knows that Hollywood stars can magnetize an audience more effectively than can any other attraction, and that such an audience responds readily to an appeal made by its popular favorites. It knows, finally, that when that intangible quality known as morale is involved, the presence of entertainment personalities is of immeasurable value. Wishing to allocate available personalities where they would do the most overall good, these leaders brought the Victory Committee into being as the outgrowth of the Hollywood Coordinating Committee for Stage, Screen and Radio.**

And that's how all those stars made all those appearances in all those locations throughout all those years of World War II: the Hollywood Victory Committee, which was established on December 10, 1941—just three days after Pearl Harbor—to coordinate all those efforts. By the end of the war, Hollywood had racked up 56,037 free appearances by 4,147 personalities in 7,700 events. Delaware accounted for a few of those.

GLORIA STUART: If you aren't familiar with some of Hollywood's stars from its Golden Age, but you still recognize the name Gloria Stuart, you most likely know her as Old Rose from 1997's *Titanic*. But the actress's career began long before that—about seven years before the start of World War II and ten years before her first of two appearances in Wilmington in 1942.

Her first visit was in May as the celebrity guest of honor at a luncheon at the Hotel DuPont to help promote the sale of bonds and stamps; the appearance was arranged by the United States Treasury Department. At the luncheon, which was open to the public and drew about six hundred people, Stuart wowed the crowd by delivering more than superficial spokesperson greetings. In her address to the audience, she said, among other things, "As civilians we have been called upon to help the war. We all can't go up in a fighter plane and shoot down six enemy craft in five minutes. We all can't have the pleasure and privilege of bombing Tokyo. I have heard grumbling and complaints…about having to curtail use of the car, walking to work or

---

* Excerpt from the "Purposes and Policy" section of the *First Yearly Report of the Activities of the Hollywood Victory Committee during the First Year of America's Participation in the War Against the Axis*

Actress Gloria Stuart during one of her two 1942 visits to Wilmington. On both visits, she promoted war bonds. *Delaware Public Archives.*

to bus and car lines. Some complain about food shortages and rationing. I think that is dreadful. I think it is dreadful because…the boys in Bataan walked thirty miles or more to fight. They ate horse meat—when they could get it. And when they went out to perform a duty, they knew not if they would return—or if they did return, in what condition…they didn't complain." After the luncheon, Stuart helped sell bonds at the Delaware War Savings Staff booth in the hotel lobby.

She returned in September for a little pleasure and a little business. On the pleasure side, she was in town to support her husband, Arthur Sheekman, who cowrote the play *Franklin Street*, which was opening at the Playhouse. But she took care of business too, taking a day to visit numerous plants in the city to promote war bond sales; to present war bonds to one plant's employees (fifty in all) who used payroll allotment to buy the bonds; and to appear as guest of honor at a YMCA luncheon, all at the behest of the Wilmington War Savings Committee. Her appearances worked, as bond sales soared at every plant she visited, and she again did not hold her tongue, stating at one stop that Japan and Italy "are out to get us; this war is a question of them or us."

Fay Wray: "It was beauty killed the beast," said Robert Armstrong in his role of Carl Denham in 1933's *King Kong*. Nine years later, that beauty, Fay Wray, found herself in the First State to promote the sale of war bonds and stamps. In August 1942, Wray arrived in Wilmington, and shortly thereafter motored to Smyrna for a luncheon and afterward a visit in Clayton; she spoke of the importance of war bonds and stamps at both gatherings. From there, she was the star attraction at a parade and war bond rally in Dover, which was to be held in front of city hall but, due to weather, was instead moved indoors to the field house of Dover High. In her address, she mentioned noticing that "Delaware" ends with "aware" and that all Delawareans should remain "aware that we are in a war. We can't be slaves to Germany." Her appearance resulted in $168,000 in war bonds being sold.

Paulette Goddard and William Gargan: Arguably the biggest star to arrive in the First State during the war was Paulette Goddard, although

As part of the "Salute to Our Heroes" event in September 1942, movie star Paulette Goddard (*center*) appeared in Dover. The woman holding Goddard's hand in the photo is Muriel Schwartz, daughter of theater owner George M. Schwartz, who had recently passed. *Delaware Public Archives.*

that was not the original plan. On September 1, 1942, it was announced in the news that Rita Hayworth would be coming to town in conjunction with the monthlong "Salute to Our Heroes" event, but two weeks before her scheduled visit, Hayworth took ill and Goddard was called up. That's some pretty good bench depth.

It was a whirlwind visit for the actress (*Modern Times*, *The Great Dictator*) that started in Pennsylvania, where she had a previous appearance, included car sickness and a police escort, then went from the state line to Wilmington to Dover, where she was in a parade that included state and local officials, a military detachment, the Delaware State Guard and Fort Miles's Harbor Defense Band. That was followed by a luncheon at the Hotel Richardson, where guests who bought a war bond could eat with the star. With her on this journey were Lieutenant B.A. Passanante, who lost his leg at the Battle of Bataan, and fellow actor William Gargan, who appeared in dozens of pictures and was nominated for a Best Supporting Actor Oscar for his work in 1940's *They Knew What They Wanted*; all three guests of honor spoke to the crowds.

Once back in Wilmington, Goddard and Company visited local war plants before being guests of honor at a $50 bond-a-plate dinner at the Hotel DuPont. The four hundred guests could buy more bonds to secure autographs, but the highlight of the evening may have been what was referred to in news items as the Chinese auction, where up for bid were Goddard's hat, gloves and compact. A Chinese auction is one where, like a traditional auction, people bid on items and the highest bid wins, but all losing bidders must still pay what they bid. Goddard's visit resulted in almost $600,000 worth of bond sales. (More information about the broader "Salute to Our Heroes" event is in "The War Loan Drives: Financing the Fight Through Film.")

GAIL PATRICK AND GENE LOCKHART: March 1943 brought a pair of Hollywood heavyweights to the First State in the name of raising money for the Red Cross War Fund Drive. One Tinseltown luminary was actress Gail Patrick, who at that point in her career had appeared in about fifty movies, including *My Man Godfrey* and *My Favorite Wife*. Gene Lockhart's résumé was over sixty titles strong, including *His Girl Friday* and *Meet John Doe*.

The pair arrived in Wilmington from Philadelphia on March 2 and wasted no time, first meeting with Red Cross representatives at a reception at the Hotel DuPont. That evening, after dinner at the Wilmington Country Club, the duo divided and conquered as Lockhart spoke to the audience at the Warner while Patrick went to the Loew's Aldine and spoke to the

Actress Paulette Goddard receives applause at a Dover luncheon. She was in Delaware for the "Salute to Our Heroes" event in September 1942. *Delaware Public Archives.*

Actress Paulette Goddard and actor William Gargan (both standing in the car in the center of the picture) in a parade in Dover as part of the "Salute to Our Heroes" event in September 1942. *Delaware Public Archives.*

Actress Gail Patrick and actor Gene Lockhart (*far left*) visit Wilmington to help raise money for the Red Cross War Fund Drive (March 1943). *Delaware Public Archives.*

crowd there. Both urged their audiences to contribute to the Red Cross, with Patrick reminding folks that 11,500 Delaware men were in the service and could benefit from even one dollar per month. The next morning, Lockhart and Patrick visited Red Cross headquarters in Wilmington before heading to Baltimore.

An interesting side story: While in town, Patrick was surprised by her brother, whom she had not seen in almost a year. Ensign Francis Fitzpatrick, a naval aviator, secured a furlough from his Texas base and flew to New Castle Army Air Base when he knew his sister would be in town. He became part of the entourage and traveled onward to Baltimore with his sister.

DEAN JAGGER AND MARY JANE WALSH: Monty Woolley, not Dean Jagger, was an advertised Hollywood star scheduled to appear at the opening of the War Bond Center at the Delaware Power & Light building in Wilmington on July 2, 1943. To that point in his career, Woolley was probably best known for his role in 1942's *The Man Who Came to Dinner*. That day he was scheduled to autograph bonds and speak to the crowd, but it wasn't meant to be. As the

Actor Dean Jagger is flanked by two WACs (July 1943). *Delaware Public Archives.*

story goes, he required a script, because apparently for all his acting prowess, he was not a gifted ad-libber. A script was sent to him, but unfortunately, he took ill and was unable to attend.

Along came Dean Jagger to take his place. Jagger, perhaps not as well-known as Woolley but certainly no less accomplished, had no script problems. In his address to the crowd, Jagger said, "It is no longer correct to say of a soldier that he has come home from the war. We are all in this war—and the war is all around us—in our offices, our shops, our playgrounds, and our hideaways." He further rallied the crowd to dig deeper into their pockets, as Delaware's bond efforts were slow at the time.

Appearing with Jagger was Mary Jane Walsh, Broadway star of, most notably, *Sing Out the News*; the Jive Bombers from NCAAB; and Fort DuPont's Private First Class Harry P. Mitchell, who reenacted Caesar Rodney's ride of July 2, 1776.

In an odd Hollywood postscript, Woolley and Jagger, now forever linked by Delaware, would go on to appear, separately, in two beloved Christmas movies. Woolley plays Professor Wutheridge in 1947's *The Bishop's Wife* alongside Cary Grant, Loretta Young and David Niven; while Jagger plays Major General Thomas F. Waverly in 1954's *White Christmas*, with Bing Crosby, Danny Kaye, Rosemary Clooney and Vera-Ellen.

THE PARADE OF STARS: In 1945, the New Castle Army Air Base was in need of $23,000 for the construction of a new service club for its enlisted men. What better way to raise money for that good cause than to have a

Rehearsing for the next night's Parade of Stars show at Wilmington's Armory in January 1945 are radio and screen stars Buddy Pepper (aka Jack Starkey) and Jane Withers. On hand to hear them are New Castle Army Air Base WACs Private First Class Salisbury and Private First Class Droztomski. *Delaware Public Archives.*

bunch of famous people put on a show? It took place at the Armory in Wilmington, it spanned two nights and it was quite something.

On Friday and Saturday, January 26 and 27, from about eight o'clock to midnight each night, the Armory welcomed a combined 4,400 people who witnessed a cavalcade of talent from radio, stage, screen and sport.

Friday Night

The Skymeisters opened the festivities with the National Anthem.

Buddy Pepper (aka Jack Starkey—see further in this chapter for more) played master of ceremonies.

Men from the New Castle Army Air Base and Army Air Base Five (Camp Springs, Maryland) competed in a basketball game.

Gypsy Rose Lee (with her "pert wiggle," as the papers called it) performed a striptease.

Leonard Elliott, a vaudevillian, stage and screen actor and nightclub comedian, entertained.

Former national table tennis champion Corporal Sol Schiff and current no. 3, Private Richard Miles, competed, with professional golfer Chick Harbert acting as referee.

Musical numbers were performed individually by concert pianist Corporal David Sokoloff, boogie-woogie pianist Lannie Scott, singer/dancer Jit Thomas, drummer Bob Sheble and singer Jessica Dragonette (who, accompanied by Sokoloff, sang five numbers, including "I Dream of Jeanie with the Light Brown Hair").

The Radio Ramblers performed a comedic Hitler sketch.

Local sportscasters Frank Denney and Herm Reitzes appeared.

Sergeant Joe DiMaggio (yes, *that* Joe DiMaggio) auctioned two baseballs: one was signed by New York Giants pitcher Carl Hubbell (fetching $25), and the other was signed by Babe Ruth, Lou Gehrig and other Murderers' Row Yankees (netting $75).

Actress Jane Withers performed a comedy routine and later jitterbugged with a random GI.

Man Mountain Dean, a wrestler, auctioned off a genuine German-issued soldier's stove (most likely an Esbit Stove) for $15.

NCAAB officers' wives collected dimes for the March of Dimes; Park Theatre manager and local March of Dimes chairman A.J. DeFiore was there to collect.

Saturday Night

The Skymeisters again opened the festivities with the National Anthem.

Buddy Pepper again played master of ceremonies.

Gypsy Rose Lee (still with that pert wiggle one supposes), performed another striptease.

Soprano Nanette Marchand, radio personalities Monica Lewis and Danny O'Neil, singer Ilene Woods (who would go on to voice Cinderella in the animated Disney classic) and (again) Leonard Elliott all performed.

Jane Withers returned, this time to do a little baseball auctioning herself. She pitched (so sorry) a ball autographed by Lou Gehrig, Babe Ruth, Jimmie Foxx and others, which scored a final bid of $225. And again she jitterbugged.

Another table tennis match was played between Schiff and Miles; Harbert again refereed.

Harbert added trick golf shots to his entertainment responsibilities.

NCAAB officers' wives once again collected for the March of Dimes.

A considerable amount of exhibition tennis was played, and according to reports, this event was the first time in the United States that amateurs and professionals competed against each other. The participants were as follows:

Opposite: Actress Jane Withers attracts the fellas at the Parade of Stars event at the Armory in Wilmington (January 1945). *Delaware Public Archives.*

Right: Actress Gypsy Rose Lee appears at the Parade of Stars event at the Armory in Wilmington (January 1945). *Delaware Public Archives.*

Alice Marble, no. 1 player in the country 1936–40
Corporal George Lott, former Davis Cup team member
Billy Talbert, he of Wilmington and the no. 2 player in the country at the time
Sidney Wood, competitor at Wimbledon and member of the Davis Cup team
Lieutenant Hal Surface, Top 10 in the country at the time
Vinnie Richards, multiple doubles championship winner
Charles Wood, American Lawn Tennis Professional Association president

(Celebrity appearances at War Loan Drives can be found in "The War Loan Drives: Financing the Fight Through Film.")

The Troop Entertainers

While the Parade of Stars was one of the splashier, non–war loan drive events to benefit a base, famous folks of various stripes made smaller base-specific appearances, too.

Peggy Ann Garner: Not all celebrities who found their way to the First State were old enough to travel alone. Peggy Ann Garner was one of those celebrities. The child star, born in 1932 and in her first film at age six, made a special visit to Fort DuPont in August 1942. Sure, her latest movie, *The Pied Piper*, was playing at the fort theater, but Garner was in town for a much more personal reason: stationed at the fort was her father, Lieutenant William G.H. Garner, and daddy and daughter had not seen each other in a year.

But because young Garner was a star as well as a daughter, her visit was more than just an emotional reunion. When she arrived in Delaware, she was escorted to the fort by Governor Bacon and some military brass, and while there, she visited the post hospital and the mess hall, as well as the post theater for a screening of her film. Throughout the day she signed autographs and posed for pictures, and it was all captured by Fox Movietone cameras. (The newsreel footage was screened a week later at the Rialto.)

Garner would make one more wartime trip back to Delaware. In December 1942, she again visited her father at Fort DuPont, but instead of screening a film, she read "The Night Before Christmas" to the children of the base.

Charlie Peterson: Entertainment took shapes other than movies and shows and song-and-dance. In the case of Charlie Peterson, entertainment took the shape of billiards. He was known as the "Missionary of Billiards" for his tireless efforts to promote the game around the country—so tireless, in fact, he suspended his professional career during the war so he would be able to tour military bases to entertain and teach the troops. The trick-shot champ and future hall-of-famer made one of his last stops at the New Castle Army Air Base in March 1944, part of 490 military base visits since Pearl Harbor.

Joe Louis: From June 1937 to March 1949, Joe Louis did something no other boxer had done before or since—held the heavyweight title for nearly twelve years and successfully defended that title an astounding twenty-five times. Within that period of time, Louis also served in the army (1942–45) and rose to the rank of technical sergeant. And within his years of service, the "Brown Bomber" made appearances in Wilmington as a fighter, a government spokesman and a fight referee (not to mention having appeared in a few films, too).

In October 1944, after touring American fronts to entertain troops in combat areas, Louis was tapped by the War Manpower Commission to address absenteeism at war plants, which brought him to Wilmington. The government and employers took absenteeism—and as an extension, workplace safety that directly affected absenteeism—very seriously. Every absent worker equated to reduced production, which equated to less support for the troops. While in town, Louis spoke on the subject to a combined audience of about twenty thousand at two war plants struggling with absenteeism, a public meeting at Howard High School and a rally at Rodney Square. At that Rodney Square rally, Louis said to every working person in attendance, "Without your help there'll be no victory, and without victory there will be no America."

A month later, Louis was back in town for an exhibition fight at the Armory, where eight hundred locals watched the champ take out Dan Biggers with a TKO in the third and final round. And in August the following year, Louis

Boxer Joe Louis meets workers at the Dravo Corporation shipyard. Louis was in town to speak to tens of thousands of Wilmingtonians about reducing absenteeism in war plants in 1944. *Delaware Public Archives.*

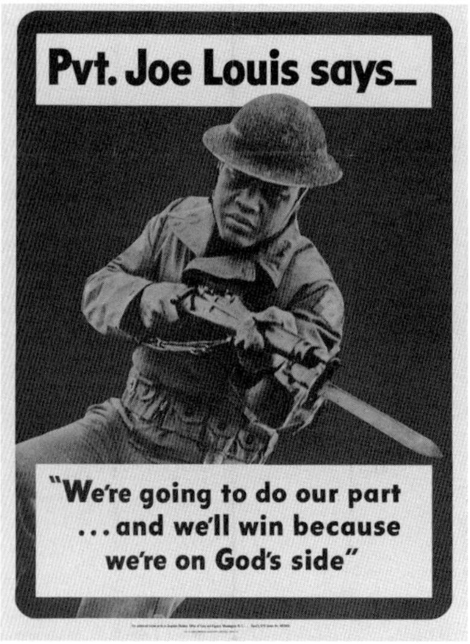

This government poster uses boxer Joe Louis, early in his military career, to stimulate support for the war (circa 1942). *National Archives and Records Administration.*

was back in Delaware, this time at the New Castle Army Air Base, to referee a bout between a couple of local boxers in front of a crowd of two thousand servicemen and civilians. (Sugar Ray Robinson was another guest referee that night.) While there, Louis also visited men in the base hospital.

And of course Louis appeared in Delaware on celluloid in the World War II era—in numerous fight pictures screened at the National Theatre; in the star-studded *This Is the Army*, which screened around the state in 1943; and in the documentary short *Sergeant Joe Louis on Tour* (1943), which followed him on his army tours during the war. But perhaps his most unique on-screen appearance was in a film called *The Negro Soldier* (1944). The documentary short, which was produced by Frank Capra, is a film aimed at recruiting African Americans into the service. It depicts reenactments of African Americans in U.S. armed conflicts dating back to the American Revolution, as well as accomplishments by African Americans in this country's history (in the arts, sports, government, education and so on).

And in what might be the oddest piece of information I have ever found, while Louis was appearing at NCAAB in 1945, he posed for a photo op of himself clipping his nails with cuticle scissors that once belonged to Adolf Hitler. As the story goes, First Sergeant Jacob Datler, who was stationed at New Castle, had found and kept a leather case containing a complete toiletry set that belonged to Hitler; the set was at Hitler's Berchtesgaden retreat.

KAY ARMEN: Charmin' Kay Armen was a stage actress who eventually made it to Hollywood and a singer for whom "Come on-a My House" was written (only for the song to find success instead with Rosemary Clooney) with almost six decades in show business. In the earlier part of that career, she flew to Delaware from New York to entertain the boys at Dover Army Air Field in August 1945.

THE VICTORY PARADE OF SPOTLIGHT BANDS: In late 1941, the Coca-Cola Company sponsored live fifteen-minute radio broadcasts of big-band music six nights a week; most of those performances were broadcast from New York, and the series was very popular. Over the course of time and the war, programming changed, and eventually those performances were broadcast from military bases and war production plants all over the country. At least four of those broadcasts came from Delaware.

One was Ted Fio Rito and His Orchestra, who played at Fort DuPont in October 1943. Fio Rito was a keyboardist, composer and bandleader whose success included two no. 1 hits in the 1930s ("My Little Grass Shack in Kealakekua, Hawaii" and "I'll String Along with You," both in 1934). He also cowrote the notable tunes "Toot, Toot, Tootsie, Goodbye" (1922) and "Laugh, Clown, Laugh" (1928). Singers who performed with his band included Betty Grable and June Haver.

A few months later, in January 1944, Andy Kirk and His Clouds of Joy entertained from the New Castle Army Air Base. Even though the band bore his name, Kirk was a bandleader from the back row, playing an instrument that didn't even warrant a solo (the bass saxophone). Instead he let singers

At an unknown location, American actress Jinx Falkenburg receives a tetanus shot from Major Joseph McDaniel Jr. of Dover (undated). *Delaware Public Archives.*

like June Richmond and Pha Terrell front the performances. Kirk had a 1942 hit with "Boogie Woogie Cocktail."

In December 1944, the NCAAB was also the spot of the third Delaware-based broadcast, when Jan Savitt and His Orchestra appeared. Savitt was a Russian-born violin prodigy whose father was a musician in Tsar Nicholas II's Imperial Regiment Band. Savitt and his parents immigrated to America when he was fifteen, soon after which he became one of the youngest musicians to play with the Philadelphia Orchestra as led by Leopold Stokowski. Gloria DeHaven was once one of his singers, as was George Tunnell, whose stage name was Bon Bon, one of the first Black singers to work with a white band.

The fourth broadcast was in Dover in February 1945 and featured none other than Count Basie and His Orchestra. William James Basie was born in Red Bank, New Jersey, in 1904, and after dropping out of junior high school he made a name for himself playing piano at local venues. Between those early years and his appearance at Dover Army Air Field, Basie toured with vaudeville troupes; studied under Fats Waller; formed his Orchestra (originally called Barons of Rhythm); cut records on the Decca, Columbia and RCA labels; married and started a family; and appeared in half a dozen films, including 1943's *Stage Door Canteen*.

The Country Servers

A few celebrities found their way to the First State not to make a sales pitch or put on a show but to serve their country.

Jack Starkey: Better known as Buddy Pepper (his show biz name), Jack Starkey was born to entertain. Deemed a musical prodigy when he learned piano by ear at age seven, Starkey would find success early, performing on stage and on radio and in movies as an actor, singer, dancer, musician, songwriter and bandleader. In the fall of 1942, Starkey enlisted to be an entertainer. However, on the same day his request was approved, he was instead inducted, but that didn't stop him from finding his place as an entertainer stationed in California. He was later reassigned to the New Castle Army Air Base, where, when he wasn't working in the mail room, he was entertaining servicemen and civilians alike and making appearances at various events, including the Parade of Stars (with his on-screen partner Jane Withers). One postwar note: Starkey would go on to cowrite "Vaya con Dios" in 1952, a song that would be immortalized by Les Paul and Mary Ford in 1953.

Private David Sokoloff plays a war bond luncheon (undated). *Delaware Public Archives.*

DAVID SOKOLOFF: Before being inducted into the army in July 1943 and being stationed at the New Castle Army Air Base, David Sokoloff was a renowned concert pianist, composer and conductor. The Philadelphia native took up the piano at age five, went on to study at the Philadelphia Music Academy and eventually became director of that academy's piano department. He was the first pianist to perform fifteen concertos in a single season with the Philadelphia Symphony Orchestra.

During his eighteen months stationed at NCAAB, Sokoloff made countless appearances around the state, performing at gatherings as intimate as military memorial services and as raucous as the Parade of Stars, with many benefit functions and bond rallies in between. In March 1945, as a corporal, he was transferred to Morrison Field in West Palm Beach, Florida.

HAL SURFACE: All celebrities may be entertainers, but not all entertainers sing or dance or act. Such was the case with Hal Surface, who was a tennis star stationed at New Castle Army Air Base in October 1944. Surface's tennis career began in the 1930s, a decade that saw him as a member of the Davis Cup team and the no. 7 player in the world in 1937; that same year, he was a quarterfinalist at Wimbledon.

Lieutenant Surface was between assignments while stationed at NCAAB, having served eighteen months in the African theater of war and awaiting an assignment to special service school in Lexington, Virginia, where he would be formally educated on the importance of sports to troops' physical well-being.

MITCHELL "MIKE" FRANKOVICH AND BINNIE BARNES: Two celebs came as a set! The demand to come to Delaware was placed on Mike Frankovich when he was named executive officer of New Castle Army Air Base in December 1944.

Frankovich had made a name for himself as an all-American football player at UCLA, after which he played pro baseball, announced sports on radio, produced films and served as Joe E. Brown's personal pilot, shuttling the entertainer to shows at 450 bases in seventeen countries during the war. (That he was also Brown's adopted son surely helped him land that gig.)

Actress Binnie Barnes and her husband, Mike Frankovich, who was the executive officer of New Castle Army Air Base (1944). *Delaware Public Archives.*

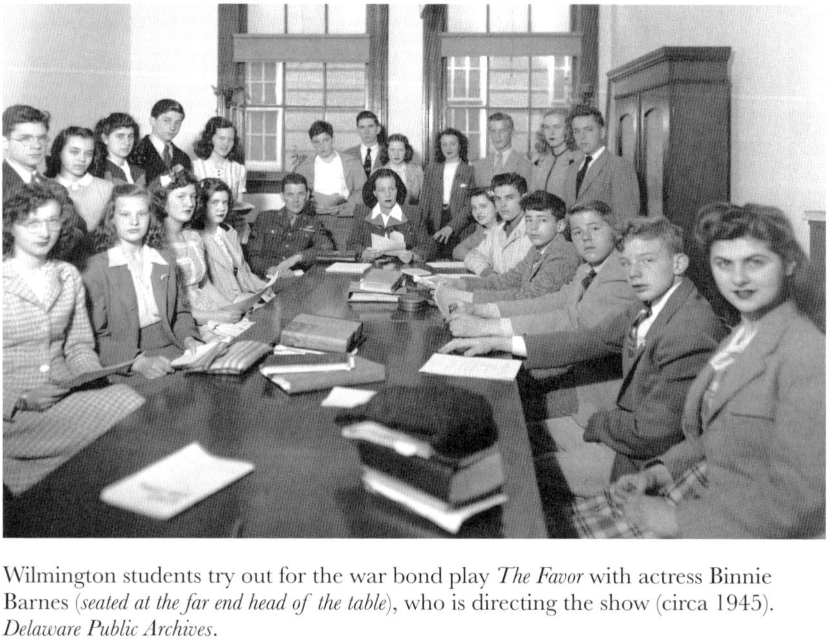

Wilmington students try out for the war bond play *The Favor* with actress Binnie Barnes (*seated at the far end head of the table*), who is directing the show (circa 1945). *Delaware Public Archives.*

His wife, the British-born Barnes, had close to fifty film credits at the start of the war, most notably 1936's *Three Smart Girls*, where she had top billing but Deanna Durbin stole the spotlight as it was her first feature film, and 1933's *The Private Life of Henry VIII*, in which Barnes plays Henry's fifth wife, Catherine Howard.

While their time living in Delaware was brief (circa December 1944–June 1945), they certainly made the most of it. Frankovich was promoted to deputy commander in March 1945, and he gave speeches at various bond and war rallies as needed. Barnes, in addition to rally appearances, took up directing local amateurs—minted as the Delaware Treasury Players—in a series of short war bond plays beginning with *The Favor*, about a soldier on leave who convinces a woman to buy a war bond instead of a fur coat. The play was performed on multiple occasions around city, with its sparseness of set and smallness of cast (three people) allowing it to be performed anywhere.

The Crowd Pleasers, Part I

And then there were the varied celebrities—varied by occupation, varied by degree of fame, even varied by species—who came here solely, or at least mostly, for the sake of entertaining the masses. In fact, when one of those celebrities came here, she came home.

Gloria Warren: I suppose the law of averages dictates that if there are enough stars in Hollywood, most larger cities will have a star from that city. Such is the case with Wilmington and Gloria Warren. Born Gloria Weiman, the fourteen-year-old singer, actress, dancer and pianist made her way to Tinseltown, accompanied by her mother, in August 1940 after graduating junior high. By May 1941, she was represented by talent agent Gummo Marx (yep, that one), was put through some formal performance training and signed a seven-year contract with Warner Bros. In July of that same year, she legally changed her name to Gloria Warren. She was considered by some to be the next Deanna Durbin.

Her first film had her third-billed behind Kay Francis and Walter Huston. The world premiere of that film—the drama *Always in My Heart*—would take place at Wilmington's newly remodeled Queen Theatre on Friday, January 30, 1942. But there were personal appearances to be had first for Wilmington's biggest celeb—four days' worth of appearances. Highlights included meeting with students from Warner Junior High (the last school in Delaware from which she graduated before heading west); receiving a

key to the city from Mayor James; manning the defense bond sales booth at Wilmington Dry Goods (where she also sang the National Anthem); riding in a parade the minute she got here; appearing before the troops at Fort DuPont (where she sang "Always in My Heart"); plus visiting the *News Journal* offices, AI DuPont Children's Hospital and the Masonic Home for the elderly. During all of this, she also conducted school studies, something she normally would have been doing in the little red schoolhouse on the Warner Bros. lot (with her lone classmate, Joan Leslie).

Opposite: Actress and Wilmington native Gloria Warren meets Wilmington mayor Albert James (circa January 1942). *Delaware Public Archives.*

Above: Actress Gloria Warren operates machinery at the *News Journal* (circa January 1942). *Delaware Public Archives.*

At the premiere, which was the first of two screenings that night, Warren was met by Governor Bacon and three thousand attendees (inside the theater and lined around the block), and in her speech to the crowd, she surprised everyone by stating she would appear at every screening the next day too, which she did.

Warren's Hollywood career started with a bang, but it didn't go very far. After *Always in My Heart*, she appeared in only five more films.

King Tarz: Who? Not who, what. King Tarz was a lion who represented MGM (not *that* lion, but one like it) on what the studio dubbed a "National Jungle Exhibition" to generate interest in their upcoming picture *Tarzan's Secret Treasure*. A motorized caravan, including a "traveling home and exhibition cage," would bring the mighty beast to theaters around the country (free of charge to the theater), and once there, King Tarz would reenact a scene from the film by walking along a twenty-eight-foot tightrope.

As luck would have it, the October 1, 1942 grand opening of Wilmington's Loew's Aldine coincided with MGM's tour plans, so after launching in front of Philadelphia City Hall, the caravan made its first official appearance at the theater's grand opening, part of a day and night of festivities at the theater that included a parade; spotlights; color guards and drum-and-bugle corps from various city schools; addresses by Wilmington mayor Albert James and Delaware governor Walter Bacon; and the appearance of Emily Allegretto, who the week prior, as part of a contest conducted by the theater, had been selected as "the typical Wilmington girl," a privilege that brought with it the title of Miss Loew's Aldine. After the parade, attention turned inside the theater, where a Pete Smith short and a Travelogue preceded the main picture, *Honky Tonk*, starring Clark Gable and Lana Turner. Gable was one of several Hollywood stars, including Mickey Rooney and Ann Sothern, to send telegrams to the theater with best wishes on its opening.

Miss America Bess Myerson sells bonds in Wilmington during the Victory Loan Drive (November 1, 1945). *Delaware Public Archives.*

The Miss Americas: The Miss America tradition began in 1921, but it hit some early bumps. It was shelved in 1928 in response to protests from religious and women's groups, and then in 1929, the Great Depression hit. An attempt to revive it in 1933 failed, but it came back to life in 1935, only to face the possibility of cancelation again with America's involvement in World War II. But the organization leaned into the times and framed Miss America as a symbol of patriotism, and the winners during the war years would go on to sell more bonds than any other public figure.

In Wilmington, a few Miss Americas made wartime appearances. Patricia Donnelly was in town in October 1939 for the grand opening of Morris Jewelers, where she also gave away twenty-inch Shirley Temple dolls as well as an autographed photo of herself to anyone who asked. In 1940, Frances Marie Burke, said to have "America's most perfect figure," received a key to the city and made several personal appearances in town, including at the Strand and Park theaters, where she sported various outfits, including bathing and evening wear.

But perhaps the most sensational visit came in 1945 when Bess Myerson, the first Jewish Miss America and the first Miss America with a college degree, was part of Wilmington's Victory Parade, before and after which she manned a booth in Rodney Square where she sold and autographed bonds.

Frances Carson: This Philadelphia-born actress made a name for herself in the New York and London theater scenes but also appeared in more than a dozen films, including three from Alfred Hitchcock: *Foreign Correspondent* (1940), *Saboteur* (1942) and *Shadow of a Doubt* (1943). Late in 1945, Carson spoke to Wilmington's New Century Club about the theater and read select excerpts of dialogue from her past stage roles. Discussions on the Victory Loan Drive occurred during the meeting as well.

The Crowd Pleasers, Part II

A lot of musical and entertainment acts came to Delaware in the war years and made stops at theaters in all three counties, putting on shows and giving people at least a short respite from the constant hum of war.

Harry Berry's Sunkist Vanities: This burlesque troupe, having been around in one form or another between at least 1932 and 1941, made a one-day-only stop at the Ace Theatre in October 1939. The ten-act team, which put on four shows that day, consisted of Harry Berry; Broadway comedians

Dr. Lewis & Stooges; Mary Keith and Her Magic Violin; Jitterbug Juggler from the House of David, Bill King; the Nonchalant Deceiver and America's Premiere Prestidigitator Willie Dee & Co.; Fanny, the Canine Prodigy; Dancing Xylophonist Roberta Hine; Rosita & Perez, Sensational Indian and Adagio; Musical Comedy Dance Stars Phillips & Breen; and the all-girl band the 7 Streamlined Sirens of Swing.

THE McFARLAND TWINS ORCHESTRA: Led by twin saxophonist brothers Art and George McFarland, this band, with songs recorded on Okeh Records, put on five shows at the Ace in late 1940.

INA RAY HUTTON: Once known as the Blond Bombshell of Rhythm, Chicago's Ina Ray Hutton made a name for herself in the 1930s as a very good bandleader of a very good all-girl band called The Melodears. But by the end of the decade, she was tired of being considered a novelty act, and she broke up the girls and recruited an all-male band. That band—and their boss lady—made a one-time-only appearance at Seaford's Layton Theatre in 1941.

HANK LAWSON AND HIS KNIGHTS OF THE ROAD: In January 1942, this group, which was heard daily on KYW out of Philadelphia, appeared one night only at the Ace. That summer, the band leased nearby Sunset Park with the intent to provide weekly, daylong entertainments on Sundays.

POLLY JENKINS AND HER PLOWBOYS: In March 1942, the Ace hosted this country-western musical group led by someone believed to be the first (and possibly only) woman to headline a country music act on the vaudeville circuit. The group had also appeared in the 1938 Gene Autry film *Man From Music Mountain*.

THE SOUTHERNAIRES: One of two all-Black groups to come to Delaware that was composed of a vocal quartet led by their pianist, the Southernaires began as a spiritual act and remained so through their tenure. In April 1942, they appeared at the Palace, then later made non-theatrical appearances at Wilmington's Walnut Street Christian Association in January 1943, selling out the five-hundred-seat facility twice in one day.

SONS OF THE SOUTH: The second all-Black vocal quartet led by their pianist/arranger to come to Delaware appeared for two nights at the Ace in January 1943. The group had begun as a spiritual act, but gained popularity and appeared on national programs when they shifted to ballads.

THE SLEEPY HOLLOW GANG: Also known as the Sleepy Hollow Ranch Gang, and with origins dating back to the early 1930s, this sextet was well known, especially in the Philadelphia area (heard frequently on WFIL), for their hillbilly music. They became so successful, they had their own country music-themed amusement park in Quakertown, Pennsylvania, where the likes of Gene Autry, Roy Rogers and Dale Evans, Wayne Newton, Carl Perkins, Frankie Avalon, Bill Haley and others performed. The Gang appeared several times in 1944 and 1945 at the Capitol, the Everett and Smyrna's Strand. Their January 1944 appearances at those venues were shortly before the group traveled overseas to entertain troops.

Max Terhune with Estel Lee and His Hollywood Cowboys: Max Terhune was a cowboy movie star with close to sixty film appearances between 1936 and 1944 who hit the road with a live comedy act in 1945. Providing his music was Estel Lee and His Hollywood Cowboys (sometimes billed as "…and Cowgirls"), a country music act with hundreds of recordings heard on radio stations around the United States. They appeared at the Capitol in April 1945.

Sons of the Pioneers: This legendary western music group played four shows at the Capitol in September 1945. One of the group's founding members was Roy Rogers (as Leonard Slye, 1933–37). The current incarnation of the group still tours today.

Ray Whitley with the Oklahoma Ranglers: Like Max Terhune, Ray Whitley was a cowboy movie star with dozens of film appearances in his career. He came to the Capitol in November 1945 with country recording artists the Oklahoma Ranglers.

Band of the Month: In February 1942, a series of live band appearances, named "Band of the Month," began at Wilmington's Armory. The inaugural event was tied to a bond drive "victory dance" sponsored by the Delaware State Federation of Women's Clubs, and the band was Tommy Tucker and His Orchestra featuring the "Swanee Sweetheart" Amy Arnell. Other bands and acts to appear throughout the series, which took place at various locations in Wilmington, included:

Johnnie "Scat" Davis (April 1942)
Charlie Spivak (May 1942 and December 1944)
Woody Herman (May 1942)
Gene Krupa (July 1942 and October 1944)
Tony Pastor (August 1942 and March 1944)
Ella Fitzgerald (September 1942)
Duke Ellington (February 1943)
Lionel Hampton (October 1943).

And Then There Was That One Time…

Clark Gable came to town! Well, not quite. It seems in April 1944 someone had themselves a laugh by spreading a rumor in the DuPont Building that the star of such films as *It Happened One Night* (1934), *Mutiny on the Bounty* (1935) and *Gone with the Wind* (1939) was spotted in the building's first-floor barbershop. For hours, the switchboards in the DuPont Building and the New Castle Army Air Base lit up with fans hoping to confirm the movie star and Army Air Corps captain was in town, but he wasn't. The closest thing was an army major who *looked* like Gable and who was staying at the Hotel DuPont.

THE EPILOGUE

The Price of Victory

Six years and one day later, it was over. What began as the German invasion of Poland on September 1, 1939, ended with the formal surrender of Japan on the USS *Missouri* in Tokyo Bay on September 2, 1945. But just because the war was over didn't mean the job was done. The United States still had a massive bill to pay down, so the country did what it had done best before: raise money. One last Loan Drive was on the horizon.

Before that, and leaning hard into the historic moment and leveraging people's sentimental desire to commemorate and collect, eight locations around the city of Wilmington offered, for one day only, special V-J Day stamps that would be affixed to bonds bought that day; the Park Theatre was one of those locations.

The Playhouse would become the lead theater in post-victory events, beginning on September 30, when it played host to the United War Fund's kickoff show for its latest campaign, "Parade of Social Agencies." (Okay, so it's not exactly "Arsenic and Old Lace.") The live show highlighted each of the agencies and their respective roles. Music was provided by the U.S. Naval Hospital Band from Philadelphia, which accompanied singing WAVES; appearances were made by singer Nancy Ness, who had appeared at the theater and on behalf of the UWF before Pearl Harbor; and USO Camp Show star Beverly Norman, who was fresh off a tour in the South Pacific and in town for the week specifically for this drive.

Victory Loan Drive poster (1945). National Archives and Records Administration.

But perhaps the biggest point of interest at the UWF show were the five pairs of nylon stockings being given away. There was a wartime shortage of nylon, but that would soon change; this was an advance chance to score what was probably the country's hottest item of that moment. The stockings were won by three women and two boys (who gave them to their mothers). It was announced at the show that $400,000 of pre-campaign donations had already been collected and would be applied to its near-$900,000 target. There was still a long way to go, with a sense of urgency because of the upcoming Loan Drive. In the end, the UWF hit its goal with about $7,600 to spare.

Sneaking in just before the start of the next (and final) Loan Drive, and to honor Navy Day, the Pike Theatre screened *This Man's Navy* in late October.

THE EIGHTH WAR LOAN DRIVE, AKA THE VICTORY LOAN DRIVE

(October 29, 1945, through December 31, 1945)

Whereas all previous War Loan Drives were fueled by motivation—to support the troops, to bolster the military, to win the war—the Victory Loan Drive (rebranded to remove "War" from its name) was fueled by celebration, and the proceeds of the drive, rather than finance the war, would help ease the debt of it. At the national level, the goal was a modest $11 billion (the second lowest of the eight drives and the lowest since the first), with the Delaware goal set at $34 million (the lowest for the state).

The first flashy event of the drive was November 1—Halsey Day—in honor of Admiral William F. Halsey Jr., commander of the South Pacific forces and the Third Fleet (and he of significant local ties). A tickertape parade in his honor drew forty thousand people to Market Street and Rodney Square that day. Four days later brought another parade—Wilmington's

Above: Two young lads with a Disney-themed bond meet Mickey Mouse during the Victory Loan Drive in 1945. *Delaware Public Archives.*

Right: Miss America Bess Myerson sells bonds to a sailor in Wilmington during the Victory Loan Drive (November 1, 1945). *Delaware Public Archives.*

Victory Parade—to the city. Miss America Bess Myerson was on hand first to sell and sign bonds at the booth at Tenth and Market Streets, then ride a float in the 3:00 p.m. parade and then sell and sign more bonds at Rodney Square. The parade was filmed.

The Victory Loan Drive continued through November. The next celebrity-featured event was a November 16 radio program that was broadcast live by the American Broadcasting Company, in front of seven hundred audience members, from the Hotel DuPont: "Blind Date," with celebrity hosts Arlene Francis and Brian Ahern, who were in town to appear together at the Playhouse in the play *The French Touch*. The game was simple—three girls (who were local) would chat up six men (three sailors and three soldiers) without seeing them; the girls would then make their picks based on the conversation. The winning couples got tickets to the play and dinner at the Hotel DuPont with Aherne. The losing men received $15, sponsor products and movie passes. All three sailors topped the soldiers, but the real winner was the Loan Drive, which took in $500,000.

The Playhouse was back in the spotlight on November 20 with a Combat Infantry Musical Show. Like most other events, bond purchases were the way in. The star of the show was the (not Delaware-based) Combat Infantry Band, a sixty-piece orchestra comprised of men who were musicians in civilian life and served overseas in the war. The band was sometimes referred to as the "million-dollar band" because of how much money in bond purchases their appearances generated. This appearance was no exception as another $485,000 went toward the Drive. This was the first Delaware stop for the band, which would play the Fort Miles Theatre, as well as locations in Dover and Georgetown, in the coming days. Another twenty-four pairs of nylons were also given away that night at the Playhouse.

After a quick shift of attention downstate to a Victory Rally at the New Waller on November 25, the Playhouse was back at it with another fashion show, this tame labeled—what else?—the Victory Fashion Show. Like the Fourth War Loan Drive event before it, this show featured local women modeling the latest styles courtesy of Wilmington retailers Braunstein's and Bird-Speakman. Another $225,000 was raised in bond sales.

At long last, all movie theaters in the state joined the fun with a December 7 Free Movie Day. As with similar events in the past, "free" meant that no ticket was necessary to see a film, but a bond purchase was. The theaters and their final "Free Movie Day" films (where available), this time for Victory and not War, were:

War bonds made great gifts (1944). *National Archives and Records Administration.*

Ace Theatre	*The Gay Senorita*
Arcadia	*Lady on a Train*
Capitol Theatre	*Having a Wonderful Crime* and *Nevada*
Crest Theatre	*Here Come the Co-Eds*
Earle Theatre	*Captain Eddie*
Edge Moor Theatre	*Our Vines Have Tender Grapes*
Grand Theatre	*Blue Montana Skies* and *Crime Doctor's Warning*
Loew's Aldine	*Getting Gertie's Garter*
National Theatre	*I'll Be Seeing You*
New Waller Theatre	*Betrayal from the East* and *Under Fiesta Stars*
Park Theatre	*East Side of Heaven* and *Imitation of Life*
Queen Theatre	*A Boy, a Girl, and a Dog*
Reese Theatre	*Don't Fence Me In* and *Why Girls Leave Home*
Rialto Theatre	*Fallen Angel*
Ritz Theatre	*Mildred Pierce*
The Roxy	*The Gay Senorita*
The Savoy	*Sleepy Lagoon* and *Steppin' in Society*
Schine's New Plaza	*Don't Fence Me In* and *Murder, He Says*
State Theatre	*Tarzan and the Amazons*
The Strand (Wilmington)	*Delightfully Dangerous*
Strand Theatre (Smyrna)	*Californy Er Bust* and *Shadows of Death* and *Song of the Prairie*
Warner Theatre	*Too Young to Know*

(For corporations, the Victory Loan Drive ended on December 8, but for individuals it ran to December 31.)

One of the last theater events of the Victory Loan Drive, and the last event formally sponsored by the Delaware War Finance Committee, was the December 10 Book and Authors Rally. This was also the last Book and Authors Rally in the country, and it earned its retirement, having raised hundreds of millions of dollars over the course of the war. It was the second time this event occurred in Wilmington, and once again it took place at the Playhouse.

As was the case with that first rally during the Fifth War Loan Drive, this rally offered up for auction items of significant literary consequence, with notable figures onstage to talk to attendees and sign their own works:

The Aberdeen Proving Ground Band gets ready for the Victory Loan Drive's Book and Authors Rally at Wilmington's Playhouse in December 1945. *Delaware Public Archives.*

This window display in the DuPont Building spotlights the special guests slated to appear, and shows many of the items up for auction, at the Victory Bond Drive's Book and Authors Rally to be held at the Playhouse in December 1945. *Delaware Public Archives.*

- John Erskine, author of *The Human Life of Jesus*
- Margalo Gillmore and Patricia Collinge, authors of *The B.O.W.S.: The Barretts of Wimpole Street*
- Returning master of ceremonies Mark Van Doren, author of *Seven Sleepers*
- Creator of Tillie the Toiler, cartoonist Russ Westover
- Dan Wickenden, author of *Running of the Deer*

William D. Morely, of Philadelphia, was the auctioneer for the night. After buying a bond just to get in, attendees could bid (by way of buying a war bond in the amount equivalent to their bid) on a multitude of items, including the following:

- The original manuscript of Gillmore and Collinge's *The B.O.W.S.: The Barretts of Wimpole Street**
- The original manuscript of Wickenden's *Running of the Deer***
- Personal letters from Fannie Hurst to Dorothy Pratt (on one of which is a red ink sketch of a lily by Hurst)
- Personal letters from Clifton Fadiman to Mark Van Doren (about how he likes Dickens's *Pickwick Papers*, among other books)
- First-edition copies of Marjorie Kinnan Rawlings's *The Yearling*, James Boyd's *Drums* and Christopher Ward's *The Dutch and Swedes of Delaware*, all three of which were signed by their respective authors and the illustrator of all three, the recently late N.C. Wyeth
- Original World War II posters and original cartoon drawings
- A complete set of Christmas Seals from 1907 to 1945 courtesy of the Delaware Anti-Tuberculosis Society, which came with a copy of *The People Against Tuberculosis—The Story of the Christmas Seal* autographed by author Leigh Mitchell Hodges and Miss Emily P. Bissell (Wilmingtonian and creator of the Christmas Seal)***

*This item fetched $1,225,000 from Continental American Life Insurance, which donated it to the University of Delaware.

**This item scored an even $1,000,000 from United Corp., which donated it to the Wilmington Institute Free Library.

***These items went for $725,000 to the Delaware Trust Company, which donated the items to the Historical Society of Delaware.

Authors, staff and the State Executive Advisory Committee have dinner as part of the Victory Loan Drive's Book and Authors Rally in December 1945. *Delaware Public Archives.*

Even though the three large bids were from corporations and the auction was held after the December 8 deadline for corporate donations, the author suspects these counted toward the final overall Drive tally because the bids would have been prearranged between the corporations and the Book and Authors War Bond Committee and either pledged or fully paid before the December 8 deadline, with the "bid" at the auction itself nothing more than theater. And let's be serious—Uncle Sam wouldn't leave almost $3 million on the table over a couple of blocks on a calendar.

There were other perks at the Book and Authors Rally, like a free autographed first edition of A.O.H. Grier's book *This Was Wilmington*, courtesy of the News Journal Company, to the first twenty-five people who bought extra bonds while there or the treat of having all five authors at the rally sign a program for anyone who spent an additional $1,000 in bonds.

Once the auction was done and the perks were tallied, the Book and Authors Rally rang up an astonishing $6.2 million in bond sales.

Wrapping theaters' involvement in the Victory Loan Drive, and thus the war efforts, were a final pair of bond premieres. At the Loew's Aldine on December 19 was Alfred Hitchcock's *Spellbound*, and at the Capitol on December 21 was *The Dolly Sisters* with Betty Grable and John Payne. That Loew's screening included first-come first-served freebies to patrons—freebies from the fields of battle, including German and Japanese war-used helmets and field jackets.

When the Victory Loan Drive was complete, final, final totals were simply remarkable. The $11 billion national goal was almost doubled, with a joyous nation raising $21 billion, a record in terms of percentage against goal (192 percent). Delaware's haul wasn't too shabby either, as the state amassed $50.5 million against its $34 million target.

Adding that to the totals across the other seven Drives, Delaware accounted for $441.7 million in bond and stamp sales for the duration of the war and the postwar party, a figure totaling almost $7.2 billion in 2022 money, and theaters all over the state, from Claymont to Delmar, were a critical part of that success.

May we never need efforts like that again.

SOURCES

Periodicals

Army: Magazine of the Association of the United States Army
Asbury Park (NJ) Press
Daily Times (Salisbury, MD)
Delaware Wave
Delmarva Leader (Seaford, DE)
Delmarva News (Selbyville, DE)
Dover (DE) Blast
Film Daily
Milford (DE) Chronicle
Morning News (Wilmington, DE)
National Herald (New York, NY)
Newark (DE) Post
News Journal (Wilmington, DE)
Radio Daily
Seaford (DE) Leader
Seaford (DE) News
Smyrna (DE) Times
Tribune (Scranton, PA)
Wilkes-Barre (PA) Record

Publications

Conner, William H., and Leon deValinger Jr. *Delaware's Role in World War II.* 2 vols. Public Archives Commission, 1955.

Delaware Federal Writers' Project. *Delaware: A Guide to the First State.* New York: Viking Press, 1958.

Donald, Ralph. *Hollywood Enlists! Propaganda Films of World War II.* Lanham, MD: Rowman and Littlefield, 2017.

Hess, Maria. *Celebrating 90 Years at the Playhouse Theatre.* Wilmington, DE: Playhouse Theatre, 2002.

Hollywood Victory Committee. *Final Report of the Hollywood Victory Committee.* Public Information Committee, Motion Picture Industry Western Division, c. 1946.

———. *First Yearly Report of the Activities of the Hollywood Victory Committee during the First Year of America's Participation in the War Against the Axis.* Industry Service Bureau of Motion Pictures, 1942.

Lee, William F. *American Big Bands.* Milwaukee, WI: Hal Leonard Corporation, 2005.

Metro-Goldwyn-Mayer. *Lion's Roar.* MGM, 1941.

Morgan, Michael. *Hidden History of Lewes.* Charleston, SC: The History Press, 2014.

———. *World War II and the Delaware Coast.* Charleston, SC: The History Press, 2016.

Morse, Jarvis M. *Paying for a World War: The United States Financing World War II.* Washington, D.C.: U.S. Savings Bond Division, 1971.

Nazarewycz, Michael J. *Historic Movie Theaters of Delaware.* Charleston, SC: The History Press, 2019.

Page, R. Brian. *Delaware in the Great Depression.* Charleston, SC: Arcadia Publishing, 2005.

Richards, Larry. *African American Films Through 1959: A Comprehensive, Illustrated Filmography.* Jefferson, NC: McFarland & Company Inc., 1998.

Shull, Michael S., and David E. Wilt. *Doing Their Bit: Wartime American Animated Short Films, 1939–1945.* Jefferson, NC: McFarland & Company Inc., 2004.

Slavin, Peter F., and Timothy Slavin A. *Delaware in World War II.* Charleston, SC: Arcadia Publishing, 2004.

United States War Finance Division. *Plays for Schools-at-War.* Washington, D.C.: U.S. Government Printing Office, 1945.

Wolfe, Charles K., and James E. Akenson. *The Women of Country Music: A Reader.* Lexington: University Press of Kentucky, 2021.

Films

Arosteguy, Susan, prod. *Hollywood Propaganda and World War II*. The Criterion Channel, 2014.

Cahn, Edward L., dir. *Main Street on the March*. Metro-Goldwyn-Mayer, 1942.

Capra, Frank, dir. *Two Down and One to Go*. U.S. Army Pictorial Services for the War Department General Staff, 1945.

De Rochemont, Louis, dir. *Show-Business at War*. The March of Time, 1943.

Ford, John, dir. *Battle of Midway, The*. United States Navy, 1942.

Office for Emergency Management Film Unit, prod. *Aluminum*. Office of Production Management, 1941.

Sharpsteen, Ben, and Jack King, dirs. *Out of the Frying Pan Into the Firing Line*. Walt Disney Productions, 1942.

Special Projects Section, Motion Picture Production Branch. *We're In the Army Now*. Army Pictorial Service, 1943.

Websites

Academy of Motion Picture Arts and Sciences, oscars.org
AllMusic, allmusic.com
American Institute for Economic Research, aier.org
Artstor, artstor.org
AV Club, avclub.com
Billiard Congress of America, bca-pool.com
Britannica, britannica.com
Broadcast Pioneers, broadcastpioneers.com
Cambridge University, cambridge.org
Chronicling America, chroniclingamerica.loc.gov
Count Basie, countbasie.com
Defense Media Network, defensemedianetwork.com
Delaware Collections, delaware.contentdm.oclc.org
Delaware's Government, delaware.gov
DelawareToday, delawaretoday.com
Delmarva Almanac, delmarva-almanac.com
Duke University, duke.edu
The *Guardian*, theguardian.com
Hake's Auctions, hakes.com
Hellenic Genealogy Geek, hellenicgenealogygeek.blogspot.com

History, history.com
Internet Archive, archive.org
Internet Broadway Database, ibdb.com
Internet Movie Database, imdb.com
JazzProfiles, jazzprofiles.blogspot.com
JazzStandards, jazzstandards.com
JDC, jdc.org
Library of Congress, loc.gov
March of Dimes, marchofdimes.org
Merriam-Webster, merriam-webster.com
Military Heritage, militaryheritage.com
Miss America, missamerica.org
MUBI, mubi.com
Musical Theatre International, mtishows.com
National Archives, archives.gov
National Museum of African American History & Culture, nmaahc.si.edu
National Park Service, nps.gov
National Women's History Museum, womenshistory.org
The National WORLD WAR II Museum, nationalww2museum.org
New York Public Library, nypl.org
Newspapers, newspapers.com
Norwich University, norwich.edu
Official Home Page of the U.S. Army, army.mil
Oregon Secretary of State Shemia Fagan, sos.oregon.gov
Playbill, playbill.com
Princeton University, princeton.edu
Roger Ebert, rogerebert.com
Rutgers University, rutgers.edu
Seaford Historical Society, seafordhistoricalsociety.com
See & Hear, National World War II Museum blog, nww2m.com
Smithsonian, si.edu
Sons of the Pioneers, sonsofthepioneers.org
Turner Classic Movies, tcm.com
U.S. Coast Guard, uscg.mil
U.S. History, ushistory.org
Variety, variety.com
YouTube, youtube.com

INDEX

M

N

P

R

S

T

U

V

W

Y

ABOUT THE AUTHOR

Michael was a kid during the era he considers the "Golden Age of Film Fandom," 1974–1989, when drive-ins, single-screeners and multiplexes were simultaneously popular; when broadcast networks and UHF stations offered steady diets of everything from classics and ripped-from-the-headlines made-for-TV movies to blockbusters and late-night schlock; and when premium cable and home video exploded with twenty-four-hour film programming. For all the movies he's seen in that time and since, he has only two regrets: missing the triple feature that closed the 1986 season at Naamans Drive-In (*The Fly*, *Aliens*, *Big Trouble in Little China*) and not saving the old *Halliwell's Film Guide* he bought at a library sale—the guide he used to track what he watched (and to help him decide what to watch next) in his early days. Like a good film fan, Michael even did his time working in a video store. Since 2000, he has written for numerous online film outlets; in 2014, he founded the MOT Film Society, where he brought classic films to the big screens of Middletown; and in 2019, he wrote his first book, *Historic Movie Theaters of Delaware* (The History Press), the definitive history of movie theaters in the First State.

Michael is married with two daughters.